P9-CJQ-103

Living STEAM

Living STEAM

with Anthony Lambert

NEW HOLLAND

First published in 2005 by
New Holland Publishers
London • Cape Town • Sydney • Auckland
www.newhollandpublishers.com

Garfield House, 86 Edgware Road, London W2 2EA, United Kingdom

80 McKenzie Street, Cape Town 8001, South Africa

14 Aquatic Drive, Frenchs Forest, NSW 2086, Australia

218 Lake Road, Northcote, Auckland, New Zealand

ISBN 1 84330 872 X

Publishing managers: Claudia Dos Santos, Simon Pooley
Commissioning editor: Simon Pooley
Editor: Alfred LeMaitre
Designer: Heather Dittmar
Picture researchers: Karla Kik, Tamlyn McGeean
DTP cartographer: Carl Germishuys
Map illustrator: Dean Bragge
Proofreader and indexer: Gill Gordon
Consultant: Anthony Lambert
Production: Myrna Collins
Reproduction by Hirt & Carter (Pty) Ltd, Cape Town
Printed and bound by Tien Wah Press (Pte) Limited, Singapore

2 4 6 8 10 9 7 5 3 1

LEFT *A train stands at Clarence Station, New South Wales, Australia.*

PAGE 1 *Dusk silhouettes the majesty of a hard-working steam locomotive.*

PAGES 2–3 *The Ffestiniog Railway's 2-4-0T* Linda *crosses the Cob.*

ENDPAPERS *The massive driving wheels of a Polish State Railways' Ol49.*

Contents

BELOW *The Mount Washington Cog Railway climbs to the summit of the highest peak in the Presidential Range of New Hampshire's White Mountains.*

Introduction

ANTHONY LAMBERT

THE MOST UNLIKELY PEOPLE FIND THE STEAM LOCOMOTIVE a majestic and moving sight. You would think that the famous children's author Beatrix Potter (1866–1943), who was a staunch defender of the Lake District landscape from despoliation by philistine developers, would have sided with her predecessor, the poet William Wordsworth (1770–1850), in taking a strong dislike to the iron horse. Far from it: 'To my mind there is scarcely a more splendid beast in the world than a large Locomotive... I cannot imagine a finer sight than the Express, with two engines, rushing down this incline' (from Kingswood Tunnel on the Highland main line in Scotland), she wrote while on holiday near Dunkeld.

It is precisely because the steam locomotive presents such a dramatic sound and spectacle when it is working hard that people all over the world have put so much time, effort and money into keeping steam alive. To see a restored steam locomotive in a museum is an aesthetic pleasure; to see it in action is a stirring experience.

In their delightfully varied ways, the journeys described in this book are the product of often heroic endeavour by those who have been infected by the fascination of steam. These people come from all walks of life, making the volunteer resources of heritage railways an engagingly disparate collection of talents and skills. Without them, few of the operations described in this book could survive, because they cannot operate on a purely commercial footing, despite the huge numbers of visitors attracted to the most successful.

The prime reason for this is the heavy cost of maintaining and restoring often unique locomotives; even if several of a type have been preserved, there is seldom scope for ordering more than a single replacement part from engineering specialists. Then there are the costs that stem from the desire for authenticity, which is what railway preservation is all about: modern radio signalling would be cheaper than mechanical signalling, but the signal box and its equipment are an intrinsic part of the atmosphere of the steam railway. Similarly, recently retired coaches from national railway systems would be cheaper to maintain than period carriages, but the more modern coaches do LITTLE for the quality of the passengers' experience.

Not surprisingly, the overwhelming majority of heritage railways are in Western Europe, North America and Australia, though the reasons behind their retention are varied. In these more affluent countries, the state has generally had to play nothing

RIGHT *In 1950, a group of enthusiasts took over the running of the narrow gauge Talyllyn Railway in Wales, marking the start of the movement to preserve working steam for future generations.*

TAL-Y-LLYN RAILWAY

more than a supporting role, providing the legal framework within which railways could operate with charitable status and apply for occasional capital grants to fund, say, a carriage shed or the restoration of a particularly historic locomotive.

Elsewhere the state has had to adopt a more proactive role, making a conscious decision that steam railways are good for tourism and therefore worthy of taxpayers' support. Some countries have been slow to realize the value of steam: in China, for example, the government wishes to see the country purged of steam traction on all but industrial lines by 2006.

In marked contrast is the attitude of the Polish government to the extraordinary Wolsztyn Experience. The opportunity to share the footplate on a scheduled steam passenger train timed to run at express speeds is unique. Several steam locomotives based at Wolsztyn depot operate various diagrams (specifying the locomotive for each train working) on the lines radiating from this major junction near Poznan. So impressed was Poland's Minister of Transport in 2001 by the local projects funded by income from the initiative that he committed the government to continue it for at least a further three years.

The idea of setting aside part of the state railway system to demonstrate steam has also been adopted in South Africa, where the branch line between the Garden Route junction of George and the coastal town of Knysna is generally worked by steam. The Outeniqua Choo-Tjoe offers views over the Indian Ocean and crosses one of the most photographed viaducts in the world, across the mouth of the Kaaimans River.

Even in the Horn of Africa, the Eritrean government has realized that the appeal of steam can help to fund reconstruction of the spectacular railway that climbs from the Red Sea at Massawa to the capital at Asmara. It has restored some unusual Italian-built tank locomotives to haul special trains for the growing number of visitors from all over the world. The combination of these Mallets – a locomotive with two sets of driving wheels, one fixed to the frame, the other hinged to turn on curves – and one of the continent's most dramatically engineered railways is attracting welcome revenue for the country's embryonic tourism industry.

Similar possibilities exist for Ecuador's principal railway between Guayaquil and Quito, which incorporates the extraordinary Devil's Nose between Sibambe and Alausi. The gradient over this 12km (7½-mile) section is 1 in 23.3 and entails a zigzag with the most breathtaking drops beneath the railway, as well as an Andean panorama of exceptional beauty. With the mountains come perennial problems with landslides, threatening the very survival of the railway. There are encouraging signs that the tourist potential of the railway may attract the funds needed for its upkeep.

Only tourism has kept alive the Old Patagonia Express, which gave Paul Theroux the title for his 1979 book about railway travel on the South American continent. The attractions of a steam-hauled excursion from the ski resort of Esquel, through the desolate wastes that once sheltered Butch Cassidy and the Sundance Kid, have saved the railway from almost certain closure.

The progenitor of all steam-worked narrow gauge railways was the Ffestiniog Railway (FR), a world away from Patagonia, though some of the Welsh migrants raising sheep there had probably been early passengers on the FR. One of the most

RIGHT *Canadian Pacific No. 2317 works a steam excursion on the former Lackawanna main line out of Scranton, Pennsylvania.*

2317
2317
2317

successful of all heritage railways, the FR was the first narrow gauge railway in the world to use steam traction, and it has an outstanding collection of original and reconstructed locomotives and carriages.

Social and economic circumstances in East Germany contributed to the survival of some delightful narrow gauge branch lines, which even before German reunification in 1990 had become tourist attractions. Although most then became part of the state railway, they were soon hived off to become semi-independent companies with varying levels of local government support.

The journey from Bad Doberan to Kühlungsborn West on the Baltic coast and the Rügensche Kleinbahn on the holiday island of Rügen are both very different in character, although located only an hour apart. However, they have one thing in common, a characteristic shared with most of the other surviving narrow gauge lines in Germany: they still perform a useful public transport function, especially the 'Molli' as the former is known. Besides being used by tourists to explore the area, locals use the railway to go to school or visit the shops.

Worsening traffic congestion and the desire to minimize car use in areas of outstanding natural beauty have given a new role to the North Yorkshire Moors Railway. Running largely through a national park, the railway is now promoted as a means of reaching the start of fine walks and has been incorporated into the district's transport network through the Moorslink ticket covering rail and bus services.

The same is true of the Chemin de Fer de la Baie de Somme, where summer automobile traffic detracts from the pleasures of the lovely seaside town of St. Valery. The trains that shuffle inland to a junction with the SNCF at Noyelles, before heading up the other side of the Somme estuary to Le Crotoy, help visitors to get around the bay as well as giving them a chance to arrive by train on the Amiens–Calais line.

Steam-hauled park-and-ride schemes are rare, but one of the US's most recent reopenings is just that. When the railway to the rim of the Grand Canyon in Arizona's Grand Canyon National Park was revived, the decision was taken to use steam rather than an uninspiring diesel locomotive. Although the Grand Canyon Railway's prime purpose was to keep cars out of the area of the canyon, it was felt that steam would enhance a visit and encourage more people to park their cars and take the train.

The Hedjaz Railway could fulfil a comparable function by taking tourists from the Jordanian capital of Amman to Ma'an for nearby Petra, the country's principal tourist attraction. At present steam operations are limited to excursions no further south than Qatrana. It would require substantial investment – on the scale of Sea Containers' operations linking Cuzco and Machu Picchu in Peru – but the train would be a much more interesting way of reaching the former Nabataean capital than the journey by road.

Since the first standard gauge steam railway was resuscitated in June 1960, at Middleton in Leeds, closely followed by the Bluebell Railway in Sussex, ever higher metaphorical mountains have been climbed by railway preservationists. But among the most remarkable feats has been the reopening of the railway that zigzags its way up the Blue Mountains in New South Wales. The railway had been closed for about 60 years, replaced by a tunnel, when work began on reclaiming this extraordinary

RIGHT *Europe's last remaining regular scheduled steam services run on the network of branch lines around Poznan, in western Poland.*

19th-century engineering work from the forest. Today it is a popular excursion from Sydney, reached by a station named Zig Zag on the line to Lithgow.

Many heritage railways are part of a broader attempt to give some idea how our ancestors lived. The Pichi Richi Railway at Quorn in South Australia evokes the atmosphere of an outback railway community, complete with workshops and substantial station buildings. The Cass Scenic Railroad State Park forms part of a wider conservation endeavour taking in other facets of a West Virginian lumber community.

Other lines are dependent on neighbouring tourist attractions: the Ostra Sodermanlands Jarnvag in Sweden would not flourish in the way it does were it not for the connecting journey on a 1903 coal-fired steamship or the attractions of Mariefred and Gripsholm Castle.

Although the larger heritage railways in Britain each carry a quarter of a million people a year, with three or four trains in service on peak days, there is never enough profit to fund all the desirable projects. How much more difficult it must be to fund, say, bridge repairs from the revenue of railways in less populous countries; the small population of Norway and modest tourist numbers mean that the service on the delightful Setesdalsbanen is sparse compared with almost any British heritage railway.

Some operations use infrastructure owned and maintained by others, such as Alberta Prairie Steam Tours, the Chemins de Fer de Provence near Nice, and Steamtown National Historic Site in Pennsylvania. This major museum is able to exercise the steam locomotives in its care on lines around Scranton.

The Mount Washington Cog Railway, still using locomotives built in the 1890s, and the Dampfbahn Furka-Bergstrecke (DFB) in Switzerland are both rack lines, offering a very different experience from conventional adhesion railways. Because of the gearing, the locomotives sound as though they are racing along at 100km/h (62mph) rather than a sedate 20km/h (12mph). The Mount Washington line was built to allow people to enjoy the views from the summit and has been performing this function since 1869, while the DFB was once part of the route of the famous Glacier Express.

The Banana Express and the Changa Manga Forest Railway both appeal to the residents of their nearby cities, Durban in South Africa and Lahore in Pakistan. They offer a pleasant means of venturing into the countryside, and neither relies on passengers who have sought out their English-built locomotives.

Perhaps the most idiosyncratic subject in this book is the Romney, Hythe & Dymchurch Railway, since it is the result of one man's passion for things mechanical, preferably if that could yield a turn of speed. 'The Captain', as founder JEP Howey was known, would have been delighted that his 381mm (15in) gauge railway was still taking children to school and pleasantly surprised that draught beer could be bought on selected trains.

If the railways in this book testify to one thing, it is that millions of people share that passion, or at least feel the reaction of Beatrix Potter, for the imposing sight and sound of a steam locomotive hard at work. Long may it continue.

Anthony Lambert
London, 2004

LEFT *Steam traction in southern Argentina, in the form of the Old Patagonia Express, survives despite the country's economic difficulties.*

The Americas

Canada

ALBERTA PRAIRIE STEAM TOURS

Anthony Lambert

IT IS HARD TO BELIEVE THAT as late as the mid-19th century the province of Alberta was comparatively empty. The suitability of the land for farming was confirmed in 1862, however, in a report submitted to the British government by the Irish adventurer and explorer Captain John Palliser. Besides assessing the fertility of the land, Palliser also made suggestions for the route of the transcontinental railway that would eventually unite Canada and take the agricultural produce of the Prairies to the coast.

It is over remnants of the spaghetti-like network of lightly laid lines across the Alberta wheatfields that the trains of Alberta Prairie Steam Tours (APST) operate. The company's base is the yard and reconstructed station at Stettler, which became a town only in 1906. From there APST operates a programme of half-day excursions over two lines: eastward over a former Canadian Pacific (CP) line to Halkirk and Coronation (81.4km/51 miles), or southward over a Canadian Northern line (later Canadian National, or CN) to Big Valley, a distance of 32.8km (20½ miles).

ABOVE *Canadian National Railways 4-8-2 No. 6060, used by APST for special excursions, waits on a siding at the APST depot at Stettler.*

RIGHT *APST 2-8-0 No. 41 waits to leave Big Valley for Stettler. The signal was used to indicate the need for stopping trains to call for passengers.*

PREVIOUS PAGES *Shay locomotive No. 11 tackles the grade to Bald Knob (the second highest point in West Virginia) on the Cass Scenic Railroad.*

ALBERTA PRAIRIE STEAM TOURS, CANADA

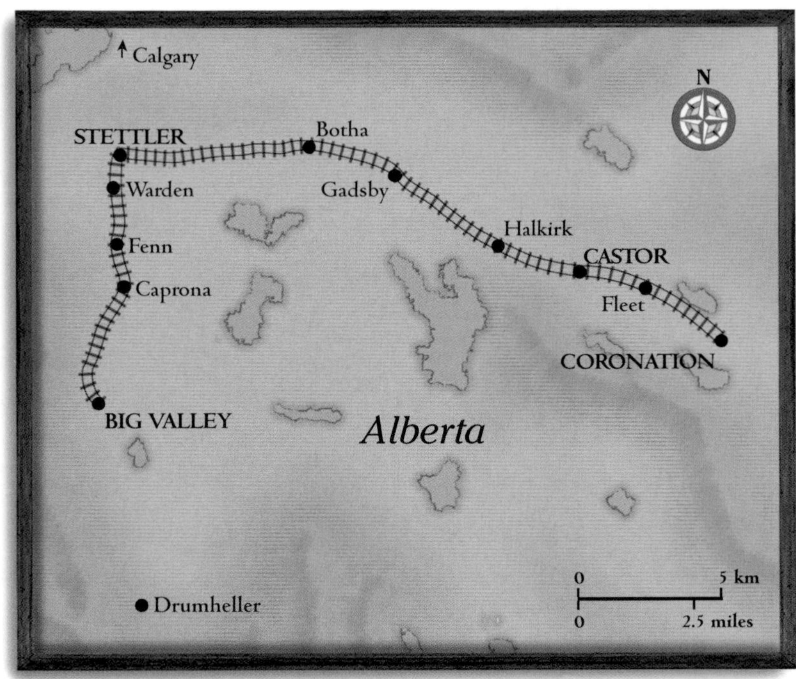

Local involvement is an intrinsic part of the trains. Not only is each excursion sponsored by a local company, but some of the enthusiastic staff are volunteers, and residents at some destinations help to provide meals or entertainment for passengers. Most excursions include roast beef dinners, and some offer a five-course meal, while others entail murder-mystery evenings and Wild West-style hold-ups.

The principal locomotive is No. 41, a 2-8-0 built in December 1920 by the Baldwin Locomotive Works in Philadelphia, for the Jonesboro, Lake City & Eastern Railway in Arkansas, finally coming to Stettler in 1990 after service throughout the American South. Less frequently used is a huge Canadian National 4-8-2 No. 6060, built in Montreal in 1944 and owned by a private society. These powerful locomotives hauled the great transcontinental express trains that ran through the provincial capital, Edmonton, situated to the northwest of Stettler.

Among the 14 carriages in the APST fleet are some used by CN on commuter trains and a former sleeping car with six-wheeled bogies which has been converted into a lounge car. Most of the carriages have been refitted and altered to accommodate such facilities as a children's play area, sales counter and bar.

The route east to Halkirk (terminus for the shorter excursions) and Coronation takes the train through flat, cereal-growing country. Once past the reversal at Payne Junction, the eye can see little but plains of wheat, while the air is filled with white balls of fluff from cottonwood trees and the fields are interrupted by traditional ochre-painted barns and occasional ponds or lakes fringed with short, white-trunked poplars. Clattering over trestle bridges spanning tiny creeks or whistling for level crossings meeting dirt roads, the locomotive, with its small driving wheels, makes easy work of the heavy coaches. Popular songs from the 1920s form the repertoire of a boatered and moustachioed tenor, accompanied by a pretty flapper, who regale passengers as they sample locally brewed beer from the bar car and watch the original source of Alberta's wealth – wheat – pass by the windows.

The train trundles through the village of Botha, which has two claims to fame: it has the oldest continuously operated store in Alberta, dating from 1907, and it was here that Canada's first manned flying machine was built, by the Underwood brothers, also in 1907. The tiny hamlet of Gadsby once rivalled Stettler in size but its population has now shrunk to less than 40, a story repeated all over the provinces of mid-Canada and frequently told in the countless tiny Prairie museums that hold the collective memory of their dwindling communities.

For a place like Halkirk, population 75, the importance of these excursions would be hard to exaggerate. It seems as though the entire community is involved in some aspect of the reception: the village hall hosts a lunch of locally reared beef, served from a series of trestle tables by half a dozen ladies; the indoor curling hall has exhibitions of local and historical interest, ranging from Indian arrowheads turned up by ploughs to photographs of the tiny one-roomed schools that once dotted the Prairies. The village store, with original bare boards, sells all manner of goods, from groceries to nuts and bolts; it's the kind of place where you feel compelled to buy something simply to support the store – I emerged with 10 years' supply of shoelaces. There is a display of sheep, rabbits, ponies, chickens and llamas; in a more grandiloquent society it would be called a 'handling collection', for

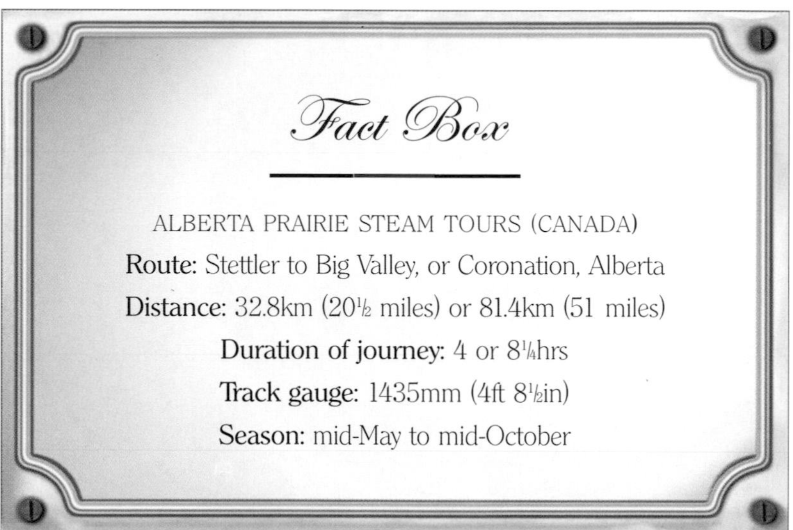

Fact Box

ALBERTA PRAIRIE STEAM TOURS (CANADA)

Route: Stettler to Big Valley, or Coronation, Alberta

Distance: 32.8km (20½ miles) or 81.4km (51 miles)

Duration of journey: 4 or 8¼hrs

Track gauge: 1435mm (4ft 8½in)

Season: mid-May to mid-October

LEFT *At Halkirk, an APST train passes the town's grain elevators, used to store wheat harvested from the surrounding grain farms.*

children are welcome to touch or hold the animals. The mysteries of grain-elevator mechanisms can be unfathomed on a guided tour of the Halkirk Alberta Wheat Pool elevator, one of a vanishing breed of all-wood construction. Sadly the distinctive outline of these immense, attractive buildings, with the name of the settlement emblazoned in huge white letters on a coloured ground, is becoming a rare sight, as local elevators are demolished and replaced by ugly, 'centralized' concrete silos of even vaster dimensions.

Beyond Halkirk, the railway continues to the town of Castor, large enough to have a golf course, hospital and a fine museum in the old station building. Journey's end at Coronation is in a town that can still boast a head-count of four figures. Some return journeys are enlivened by a 'hold-up', with half a dozen mounted hoodlums chasing the train and forcing it to a stand, whereupon they encourage passengers to part with their money – in the name of a local charity.

The southerly route ventures into hillier country, towards southern Alberta's badlands, and is very different in character from the Coronation line. Acres of yellow wheat or malting barley are interspersed with fields of Angus, Hereford, Charolais and Limousin cattle, and there is even some market gardening. Deer may be seen, and ducks and geese are plentiful near sloughs and marshes. Just south of Stettler is Warden Junction, where the locomotive and repair shops of APST are located, watched over in season by rare Rocky Mountain bluebirds, which have been attracted to the area by wooden nesting boxes along the fence lines. Sanctuary for other birds is provided by artesian-fed areas of water; any similarity to the Fen landscapes of eastern England had no bearing on the name of the next settlement – Fenn – since it was named after an official of Canadian National Railways. Dating from 1911, its Canadian Northern station building is a reminder of the remarkable degree of standardization applied to station design across the country. Also surviving is Fenn's general store and post office, bringing to mind Winston Link's evocative photograph of the store interior at Vesuvius on the Norfolk & Western Railway, with a group of customers clustered around the stove exchanging gossip while a train thunders past outside.

Leaving Fenn, trains begin their descent into the wide, sweeping valley flats known as Big Valley, where scattered well sites provide evidence of the gas and oil discoveries made here in the 1950s. The train crosses a wooden trestle bridge before reaching its destination at Big Valley station, which dates from 1912 and is now the headquarters of the Canadian Northern Society, with a display of railway artefacts and photographs. Nearby are the remains of the 10-stall roundhouse and turntable, where 14 locomotives were once based, as well as two CN baggage cars now used as part of the museum display.

The line used to extend further south through Rowley – known as Rowleywood because of the number of films shot in this period hamlet – to Drumheller, famous for the Royal Tyrell Museum, which displays remains of the many dinosaurs unearthed in the region. It is the intention of the East Central Alberta Heritage Society to raise enough funds to re-lay the track over the railbed to Rowley and eventually to Drumheller; the route of the line has already been saved through collaboration with Trailnet and its trail construction programme across Canada. Perhaps the sound of a steam whistle will again be heard in one of Alberta's most popular tourist destinations.

HULL–CHELSEA–WAKEFIELD STEAM TRAIN

Pierre Home-Douglas

North of the Ottawa River, 160km (100 miles) west of Montreal, the Canadian landscape changes from low, flat farmland to the rolling hills, lakes and rivers that characterize half of the country's 9.84 million sq km (3.8 million sq miles). This is the start of the Canadian Shield, an region of exposed Precambrian rock that stretches all the way north to the Arctic Circle and as far west as the Rocky Mountains. It is along the edge of this vast area that the Hull–Chelsea–Wakefield Steam Train makes its 64km (40 mile) journey.

The train runs from May to October, though the countryside it passes through is beautiful at just about any time of the year. But many would say that its most spectacular period is during early autumn, when the leaves change colour from green to a brilliant array of oranges, reds and yellows, saturating the countryside with a glorious glow. Visitors book months in advance for one of the peak weekends – usually around mid-October.

The trip starts in Hull, Quebec, across the river from Canada's capital, Ottawa. As the 1.30pm departure time draws near, you can hear a mix of French and English chatter as people take their seats. With a couple of toots of the train's whistle and a cloud of billowing smoke, the *train à vapeur* (as 'steam train' is known in French), pulls out of the station. The backdrop offers a strange contrast – the smoke drifts over the roofs of car dealers and fast-food outlets and a scene typical of North American urban sprawl. Soon, however, the world of asphalt and concrete is left behind as the train enters the woods of Gatineau Park and

ABOVE *The manufacturer's plate of No. 909 proclaims its Swedish provenance. The locomotive hauls a rake of coaches also built in Sweden.*

RIGHT *Shortly before the* train à vapeur *leaves Hull station, two railway workers take a last-minute coffee break.*

HULL-CHELSEA-WAKEFIELD STEAM TRAIN, CANADA

chugs up One Mile Hill. The name is a bit of a misnomer. It is actually three times longer than a mile. During a caterpillar invasion in the 1940s, trains had trouble making their way up the 1 in 20 grade; the millions of insects covering the tracks made the surface extremely slippery for steel wheels on rails.

A bilingual guide in each car provides a running commentary on the scenery and the history of the train. The line was laid down beginning in the 1890s and ran originally to Maniwaki, Quebec, a former lumber town 160km (100 miles) to the north. From the 1920s to the 1940s the route was popular with commuters and skiers, who ventured north to enjoy the ski trails in the Gatineau hills. Canada's longest-serving prime minister, Mackenzie King (1874–1950), used the train to escape to his weekend home, Moorside Cottage on Kingsmere Lake, a few miles west of the rail line. It was there that King entertained such guests as Charles Lindbergh and Winston Churchill, and it was there that he died. The Kingsmere estate is now a national historic site.

Ridership declined in the 1950s and regular passenger service ended in January 1963. The track continued to be used for freight traffic, but that also stopped in 1984. Meanwhile, a steam excursion had begun running from Ottawa's Museum of Science and Technology to Wakefield – the forerunner of the Hull–Chelsea–Wakefield Railroad, which began operations in 1992.

BELOW LEFT *The manual turntable at Wakefield is so finely balanced that two workers can spin the locomotive around in under three minutes.*

BELOW RIGHT *On the return trip to Hull, the train winds its way along the main street of Wakefield, past stores, gift shops and restaurants.*

Today, the nine passenger cars are pulled by steam engine No. 909, a 1907 Swedish-built type 2-8-0 locomotive – the only European engine to run on Canadian rails. The coaches were built in Sweden in the 1940s, and the train can carry up to 528 passengers. Each of the cars has a different name – for example, *Gatineau, Hull* and *Quebec* (which has a souvenir shop). The *Grey Owl* coach was named after the famed conservationist and author who was the subject of a 1998 film with Pierce Brosnan in the title role. Engine No. 909 also made an appearance in the film, in a scene that showed Grey Owl travelling by train during the 1930s.

Beyond One Mile Hill, the train soon reaches the western bank of the Gatineau River, which it follows all the way to Wakefield. The river played an important role in the history of both Canada and Britain. Logging in the surrounding countryside started as early as 1806. In the first years, lumber was shipped back to England to help construct ships that would battle Napoleon's navy. Later, the logging business provided an important stimulus to the nascent Canadian economy. From the beginning, the river served as the conduit for shipping the logs downstream to lumber mills. The log drives stopped only in 1992, by which time they had had a disastrous effect on the ecology of the river. Over the years, acid leached from the bark of the trees destroyed most of the plant and fish life. Today, though, the river seems to be making a recovery – as the presence of fishermen in boats attests.

The train follows the sinuous course of the river, passing numerous summer cottages that hug the shoreline. Here and there, seaplanes are moored and wooden swimming rafts lie tethered offshore. Tree-lined lanes lead down to the rail line from nearby Highway 105. Families appear from their homes and wave to the train as it passes by. On the opposite bank of the river, the Gatineau hills fade into the distance. The clickety-clack of the wheels creates a rhythmic background sound,

occasionally punctuated by the hooting of the train whistle. The speed the train travels – a stately 48kph (30mph) – is fast enough so you never tire of the vistas, and slow enough to keep you wondering what lies beyond the next bend.

A couple of troubadours entertain passengers with songs about the history of the area. The language switches from French to English as they tell tales about miners, loggers and others whose lives have been intertwined with the Gatineau River. During the summer months, the steam train also offers a Sunset Dinner Train trip, complete with a meal catered by Hull's renowned French restaurant, Café Henry Burger.

The train's northern terminus is the quaint riverside town of Wakefield, where one of the highlights of the trip takes place. To turn the 95-tonne (93-ton) locomotive around, the engineer drives it onto a large turntable that is spun around by hand by a couple of train employees – the only manually operated train turntable in Canada. The two-hour stop in the town gives passengers plenty of time to explore, and Wakefield is well worth the visit. Guides from the train offer several historical tours of the town, the main street of which is lined with shops, cafés and bistros. Near the centre of town stands the Black Sheep Inn, one of the best spots in eastern Canada to hear blues and folk singers. A short side trip down Mill Street leads to the Wakefield Mill, a riverside mill built in 1838 which now operates as an inn and restaurant. The town is also right on the Trans Canada Trail, a 17,600km (11,000-mile) recreation trail that runs from the Atlantic to the Pacific and Arctic Oceans.

Some passengers pause to peek inside the locomotive. Engineer John Bryant comments on the controls and points to two glass covered gauges in front of the boiler. 'When you step onto the steam engine the first thing you look at is the water level in them. That shows how much water there is in the boiler. It has to be above the level of the crownsheet. Nothing else matters.' The Lancashire native owns a fully

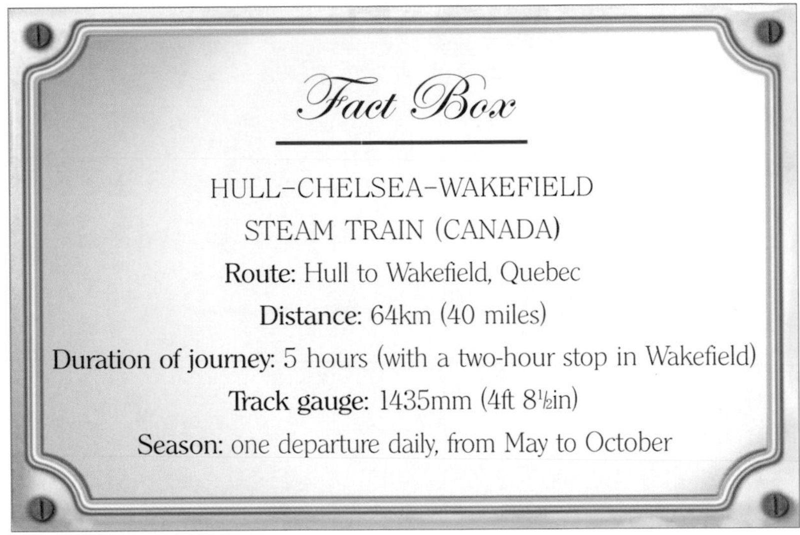

Fact Box

HULL–CHELSEA–WAKEFIELD
STEAM TRAIN (CANADA)

Route: Hull to Wakefield, Quebec
Distance: 64km (40 miles)
Duration of journey: 5 hours (with a two-hour stop in Wakefield)
Track gauge: 1435mm (4ft 8½in)
Season: one departure daily, from May to October

operational, 184mm (7¼ inch) gauge model of a locomotive that runs on the Bluebell Railway in Sussex, England, and occasionally works on that line.

After a two-hour stop, the train begins its return trip back to Hull. There is a sense of anticipation and a keenness to see how the fading light of day will subtly alter the views. But that is also mixed with more than a trace of wistfulness. Soon, too soon, the journey into the glorious past of railway travel in Canada will come to an end.

BELOW LEFT *Wakefield Mill is popular with photographers and painters, as well as visitors seeking a fine meal at its French restaurant.*

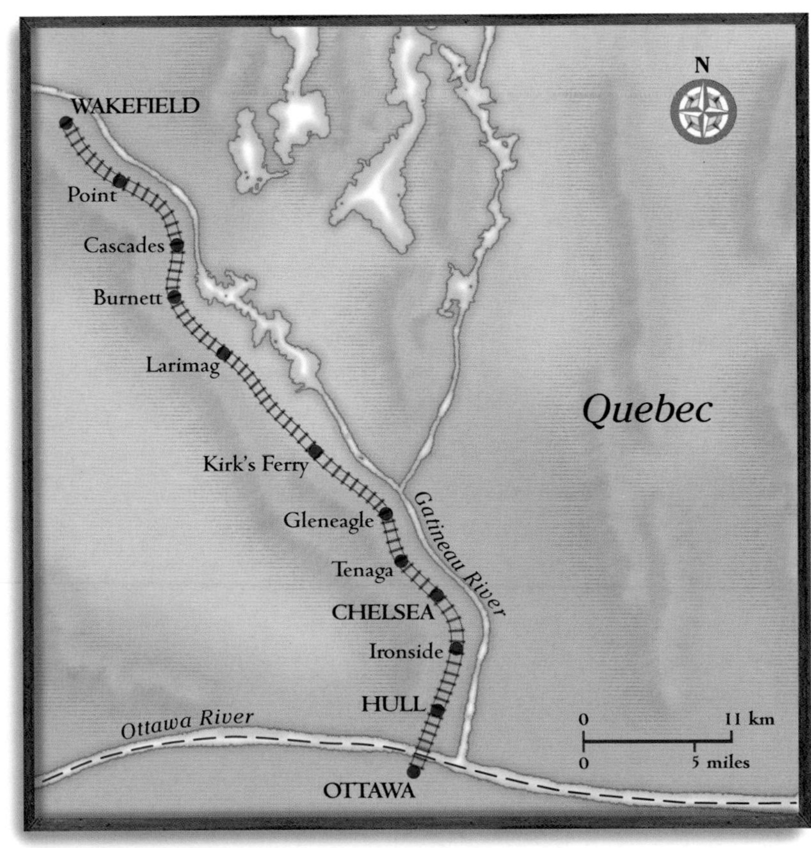

United States

CASS SCENIC RAILROAD

Steve Barry

IT'S EARLY IN THE MORNING AND THE SUN IS BURNING OFF THE MIST over the valley of the Greenbrier River. You walk down to the kitchen of your small white house and put on a cup of coffee and start preparing breakfast. Outside your window, you can see the other houses on your street, all alike, all painted white, all built for the employees of the town's lumber mill. In the distance, a steam locomotive whistle echoes through the hills. You are an employee of the Mower Lumber Company in 1950, ready to begin a day's work, right? Not quite. Actually you are a 21st-century tourist staying in the restored company town of Cass, West Virginia, and today you are going to ride a steam-powered train to the top of Bald Knob, the state's second-highest mountain.

The Mower Lumber Company operated the wood-cutting industry in the forests surrounding the town of Cass until 1 July 1960. When the mill and the railroad that served it shut down, it looked like Cass would become just another ghost town. But the state of West Virginia purchased the entire town and railroad just two years later, on 10 July 1962, and by June 1963 trains were once again running to the top of Bald Knob. Ultimately, the line would become today's Cass Scenic Railroad State Park, nestled adjacent to the Monongahela National Forest.

ABOVE *The vertical cylinders and rods give the Shay locomotive its sure-footed power to move heavy trains over rough terrain.*

RIGHT *Shay No. 2 passes the water tank in Cass before heading up Bald Knob. The remains of the Mower Lumber Company mill can be seen at left.*

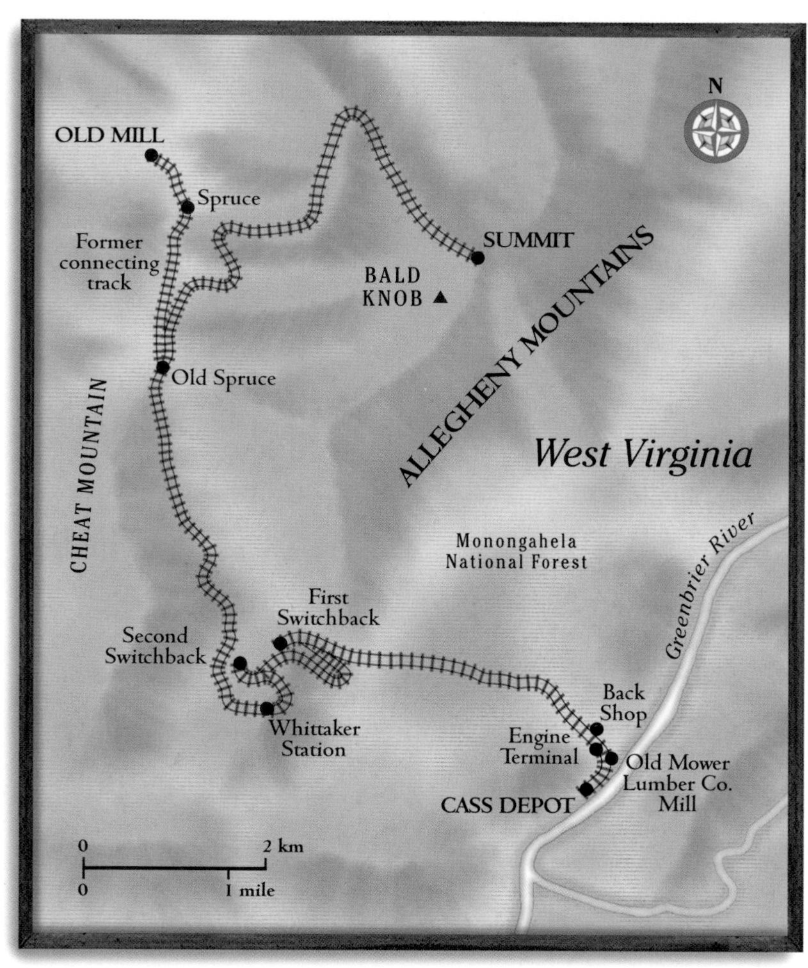

Cass is a town out of the past, a completely preserved company town built around the lumber mill established in 1902. Before you board the train for the 18.5km (11½-mile) trip into the Allegheny Mountains, take some time to walk around the town. The school, the mayor's house and the jail all still stand, albeit in various states of disrepair awaiting funding for restoration. Neat company houses line the boardwalks. Soon you'll wander past the large company store where the Mower employees bought everything they could possibly need – today you can purchase souvenirs of your visit here. A visit to the Cass Showcase, located near the store, will show you what each building in town was used for – it's well worth a look.

Down the hill is the depot. The logging railroad never operated passenger trains, but the Chesapeake & Ohio Railroad (C&O) operated a route through Cass and a station was established in the town. The original station fell victim to arson in the late 1970s, but an accurate replica now stands in its place. Soon your train backs into the station, the steam locomotive propelling several several open and semi-open cars. The cars you'll be riding in are all converted from old logging flatcars.

Now take a look at your locomotive. This steam engine is like no other you have seen before. Instead of having cylinders on either side with rods connected to large wheels, this locomotive has cylinders mounted vertically on just one side, with piston rods connecting to a drive shaft running along the locomotive's right-hand side. This drive shaft is connected to small wheels – quite different from the large-drivered steam locomotives you see elsewhere! This is a Shay locomotive, developed by Ephraim Shay in 1877 specifically for use on logging railroads. Often the tracks used by loggers were laid down only temporarily, with little grading, and were quite uneven and climbed steep grades. The Shay locomotive, with all six axles powered by the drive shaft, is a sure-footed beast, not much for speed but able to negotiate the worst track. The Cass Scenic Railroad, heir to the Mower Lumber Company Railroad, has brought in Shays from across the United States to power the trains. If you are lucky, you might get the 'Big Six' – Shay No. 6, built in May 1945 for the Western Maryland Railroad. At over 152 tonnes (150 tons), it's the largest surviving Shay locomotive in the world.

Soon your trip gets under way. The first significant sight you'll see is the remains of the Mower Lumber Company mill which, like the original depot, was destroyed by fire. The locomotive pauses beneath the massive water tank, which Cass once shared with the C&O, for one final drink before heading up the mountain. After leaving the tank, there is a modern repair shop complex where the railroad's steam power is maintained. Cass suffered a series of fires in the late 1970s, some of quite suspicious origin, and the original shop building was yet another victim of the flames.

It isn't long before the train is into the woods. The whistle blows for the crossing of Back Mountain Road, and the tracks cross Leatherbark Creek twice. The train makes a second crossing of Back Mountain Road, and that's the last paved road you'll see for the rest of the trip – for the next 16km (10 miles) you'll be roughing it.

The locomotive pushes the train into the woods – this is done to keep the locomotive on the downhill end of the train most of the time. This makes the ride to the top of Bald Knob as safe as it can be. It also makes it as clean as can be: the Shays burn coal, which produces cinders from the smokestack. With the locomotive

LEFT *Three Shay locomotives in the yard at Cass prepare to take trains up the steep slopes of Bald Knob. Cass Scenic Railroad has one of the largest active fleets of former logging locomotives in North America.*

pushing the train, the cinders fall away from the passenger cars. Locomotives are frequently run ahead of the train for special photography trips, however, when groups of rail buffs charter the entire railroad to take photos of the Shay locomotives.

Soon you reach the first switchback. These were used to help the railroad gain elevation in places where it was impractical to build a long uphill curve. The train clatters across the turnout and, once the locomotive is clear, the train stops and a trainman throws the switch. The train then backs up (with the locomotive now leading) and heads up a different track. You can really hear the locomotive work, and those in the open cars will notice black cinders falling on their heads.

The train emerges from the woods briefly, revealing a panoramic view of the Greenbrier Valley. This is Gum Field, named for the Gum family, owners of the farm in the valley. Soon the train reaches another switchback, and reverses direction once again. The locomotive will push the train for the rest of the trip.

The first stop of the trip where passengers can detrain is at Whittaker, 7.25km (4½ miles) from Cass. At this location can be seen a fine display of logging equipment, including a 'skidder'. This is a rail car equipped with a mast that can extend up to 18m (60ft) into the air. Cables from the top of the mast were stretched into the woods for a quarter mile or more, and felled timber was attached to the cables to be dragged to the railroad for transport back to the mill. This technique allowed timber to be harvested at locations the railroad couldn't reach and reduced the need to lay more track. A camp car served as a home away from home for loggers, who would live in these railcars for a week, returning to Cass for the weekends.

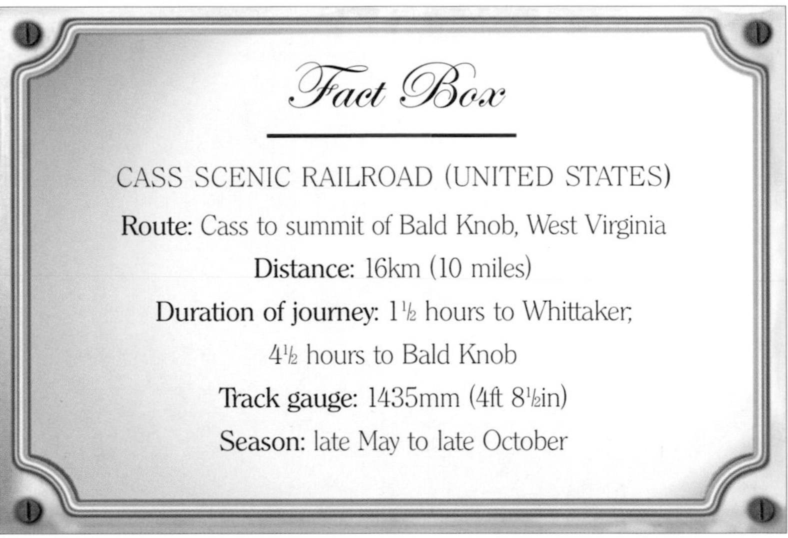

Fact Box

CASS SCENIC RAILROAD (UNITED STATES)

Route: Cass to summit of Bald Knob, West Virginia

Distance: 16km (10 miles)

Duration of journey: 1½ hours to Whittaker, 4½ hours to Bald Knob

Track gauge: 1435mm (4ft 8½in)

Season: late May to late October

Departing Whittaker, the locomotive works hard as the tracks continue uphill. You will notice that the locomotive's rapid exhaust makes it sound like it's going quite fast, but the train is actually moving slowly – 19kph (12 mph) or less. This is a function of the design of the Shay locomotives. Their low gearing made them workhorses on the hills, but fast running is something they weren't designed to do.

At milepost 6, the woods open up again for a view back into the valley towards Cass. Otherwise, you are running through the woods that have regrown since the Mower Lumber Company stopped cutting trees. The scenery is especially beautiful in October, when autumn brings reds and yellows to the leaves.

At a location called Old Spruce (not much to mark it other than a sign), you'll notice a spur track heading down the hillside. This was the connection to the Western Maryland Railway at Spruce, once the highest town in the eastern United States at 1174m (3853ft) above sea level. In its heyday, Spruce boasted a railroad maintenance shop and several houses, but only foundations remain. You can see the Spruce site through the woods a little farther up the tracks. Interestingly, the old Western Maryland tracks down in the valley are now used by another tourist railroad.

The train makes a second water stop, this time at Oats Run. There is no water tank here, just a storage tank in the riverbed and a hose. Shay locomotives were designed to draw water directly from tanks like these (or even directly from streams) using suction. Once the thirsty Shay is satisfied, it's on the road again.

Finally you arrive at Bald Knob, 1470m (4842ft) above sea level. (By comparison, Cass lies at 747m/2452ft.) Here you can detrain to enjoy a panoramic view of the West Virginia countryside. From the wooden observation deck, you can see the radio telescopes of the National Radio Astronomy Observatory in the town of Green Bank below. It's a truly breathtaking view as you can see for miles up and down the valley.

Soon it's time to reboard. The Shay will lead your train back down the hill, a lot more quietly than it came up! Kick back and relax. Close your eyes and imagine what it was like to be a lumberjack. With the Cass Scenic Railroad and the restored town, your imagination doesn't have to wander very far.

GRAND CANYON RAILWAY

Steve Barry

To preserve the scenic wonders of the nation, the United States of America started setting aside spectacular natural areas in 1864, with Yosemite Park in California becoming the first 'national park'. On February 26, 1919, the Grand Canyon in northern Arizona was added to the list of national parks, and today nearly four million people visit the site annually. The Grand Canyon is a good example of the dilemma faced by the National Park Service (NPS) at many of the sites it administers: how to keep the park available to visitors while preserving its natural environment. A partial solution to the dilemma can be found at the railroad station at Williams, Arizona, some 96km (60 miles) south of the canyon.

The history of America's national parks is closely linked with the western development of the railroads. The Union Pacific (UP) and the Northern Pacific (NP) built rail lines to newly established parks, and in many cases built the first large lodges to accommodate tourists (who arrived by train). The UP tapped into Yellowstone, Zion and Bryce National Parks, while the NP operated its own route into Yellowstone; in fact, it was trestle builders from the NP who built the classic lodge near the park's famed geyser, Old Faithful.

ABOVE *Grand Canyon No. 18 sits in front of the El Tovar Hotel at the South Rim of the Grand Canyon. The El Tovar opened in 1905.*

RIGHT *Two Grand Canyon locomotives race across the Arizona desert just before sunset on the way back to Williams.*

The Atchison, Topeka & Santa Fe Railroad (usually called simply 'the Santa Fe' and now a part of railroad giant Burlington Northern Santa Fe, or BNSF) developed an extensive network between Kansas City and Los Angeles. Wanting to get a share of the western tourism boom, the Santa Fe looked at a freight line that extended from its main line at Williams to Anita, 72.5km (45 miles) to the north. This line, built in the late 19th century, was used to transport ore from mines near Anita. The Santa Fe acquired the line and extended it the remaining 32km (20 miles) to the Grand Canyon in 1901 and began development of the canyon's south rim. The stately El Tovar Hotel was finished in 1905.

For the next 67 years, the railroad hauled passengers to the canyon, but declining ridership brought on by the use of the automobile forced the railroad to terminate passenger service in 1968. Sporadic freight service continued until 1974, when the Santa Fe officially abandoned the line. A series of private operators purchased it, but they ran into financial problems and began scrapping the railroad in 1989. However, private entrepreneurs Max and Thelma Biegart made a last-ditch attempt to purchase the railroad (which proved successful) and scrapping was replaced by restoration. On 17 September 1989, exactly 88 years after the first train arrived at the canyon, a steam locomotive once again hauled passengers to America's greatest natural wonder.

The new service started with a small 2-8-0 steam locomotive that originally ran on the Lake Superior & Ishpeming Railroad in Minnesota. It wasn't long before the number of visitors exceeded the locomotive's hauling capacity, so the railroad purchased a burly 2-8-2 that had originally worked for the Chicago, Burlington & Quincy. After a major rebuilding, No. 4960 became (and remains) the Grand Canyon Railway's primary motive power.

A ride on the Grand Canyon Railway starts at the Williams depot, which was built by the Santa Fe in 1908. Adjacent to the depot is the Fray Marcos Hotel, also built by the Santa Fe and now operated by the Grand Canyon Railway. The Fray Marcos is the perfect place to stay to get the complete historic experience. Departing from Williams (elevation 2057m/6750ft), the train passes the railroad's workshop complex where you will see several locomotives in various stages of restoration. Just beyond the shops, the train passes under the Santa Fe's busy freight main line – it's not uncommon to see a modern freight train soaring over the vintage steam train as you head north.

There are several classes of ridership available on the Grand Canyon Railway. The most economical is coach, which will get you a comfortable seat for the journey that lasts over two hours in each direction. There is also an extra-fare dome car on the train, which furnishes a panoramic view – especially worthwhile for the northern end

OPPOSITE *Grand Canyon No. 4960 halts on a short trestle just north of Williams on a cool autumn night. Occasionally, runs are made through the desert after sunset when the sky lights up with stars.*

of the line – as well as good views of the steam locomotive leading the train. Premium service is offered in the observation car, which includes food service and a platform at the back of the train for open-air riding.

It may look like desert flatlands outside your window, but looks can be deceiving. The train actually descends a steady grade for the first 56km (35 miles), although there is one steep uphill climb on this stretch that will test the locomotive's pulling power. Inside the train, singing cowboys pass from car to car performing musical selections from the Old West. Drinking water is readily available and is recommended, as dehydration can be a problem as you pass through the desert.

At the town of Willaha (don't blink – this ghost town has only one building left standing), cliffs appear ahead of the train. These cliffs are actually the north rim of the Grand Canyon, which is almost 305m (1000ft) higher than the train's destination of the south rim. Out of Willaha, the train starts to make a steady climb up Anita Hill to the location of the old mines that were the reason the railroad was built in the first place. Beyond Anita, where freight service was never envisaged, the uphill climb gets really steep as the train passes over a series of 'stairstep' grades to reach Apex, 84km (52 miles) from Williams. The scenery then changes from prairie to canyons as the train snakes its way through the short but scenic Coconino Canyon. Finally, the train arrives at the South Rim of the canyon, at the station built by the Santa Fe. During the trip, the train dropped nearly 305m (1000ft), from Williams to Willaha, then rose 366m (1200ft) to the canyon station, with steep grades all along the route.

Once the train arrives at the canyon, shuttle buses are available to take visitors to a number of overlooks along the South Rim, and the locomotive is serviced and watered in preparation for the southbound trip. A visit to the El Tovar Hotel, located on the hill behind the station, is certainly a priority during the layover. The train remains here for about four hours, but visitors can also arrange to stay overnight at the South Rim and take a train back to Williams at a later date.

The Grand Canyon has been, quite simply, overrun by visitors. The National Park Service, custodian of the nation's parks and wilderness areas, has had to eliminate the use of automobiles within the park, so all visitors must board shuttle buses or bring good walking shoes to get around. Cars can still get within walking distance of the rim, but all the overlooks are restricted to buses only. The NPS would like to push automobiles further away from the rim, and the Grand Canyon Railway is seen as offering the potential to achieve this goal. It is hoped that someday huge parking lots can be built away from the rim, and a new light rail (trolley) line can be built from the parking lot into the park.

Today the Grand Canyon Railway hauls more passengers than the Santa Fe ever did. Estimates say that the railroad keeps 50,000 automobiles out of the park each year, helping to reduce pollution and congestion. With 150,000 annual riders, the railroad has also improved the status of the town of Williams as the gateway to the canyon, as most riders use the town's hotels for their overnight stays. And the railroad, with its locomotives from the past, is seen as a key ingredient in the future of the Grand Canyon National Park.

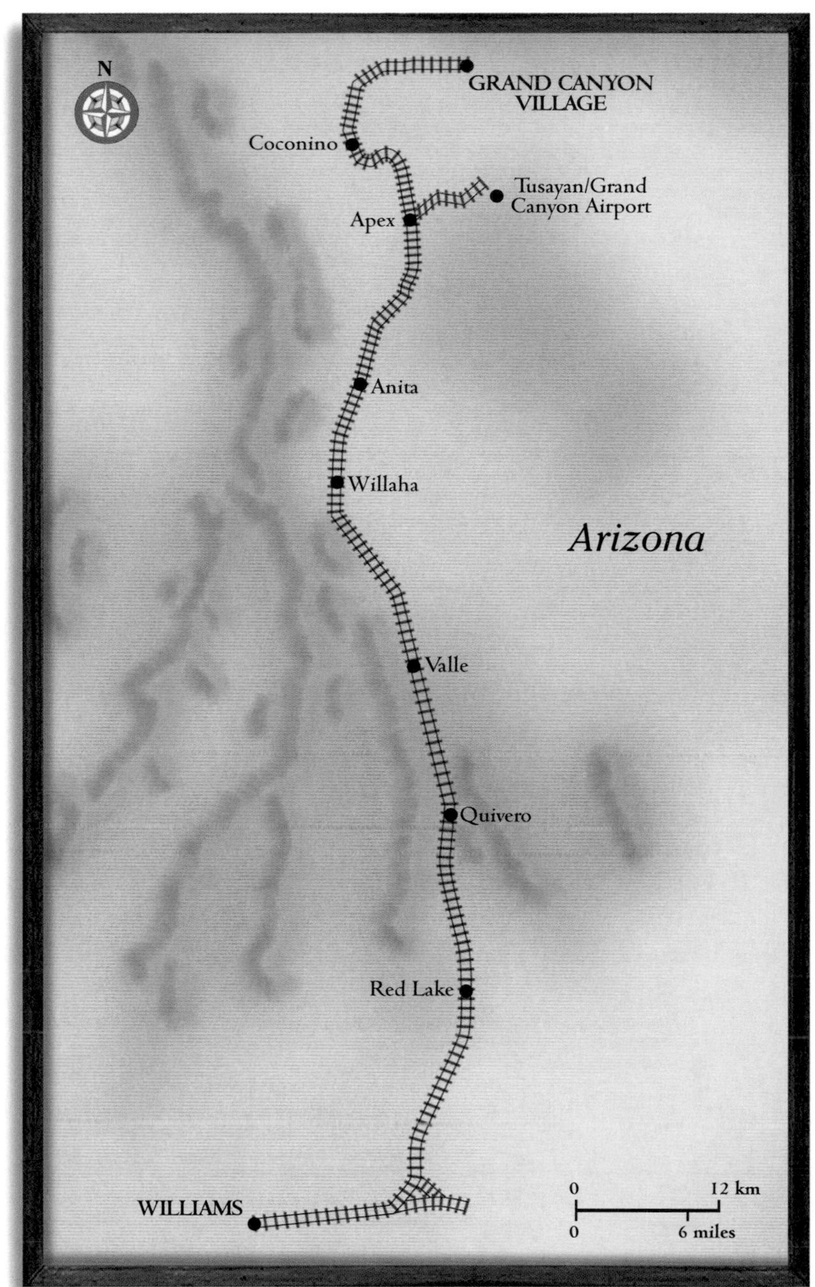

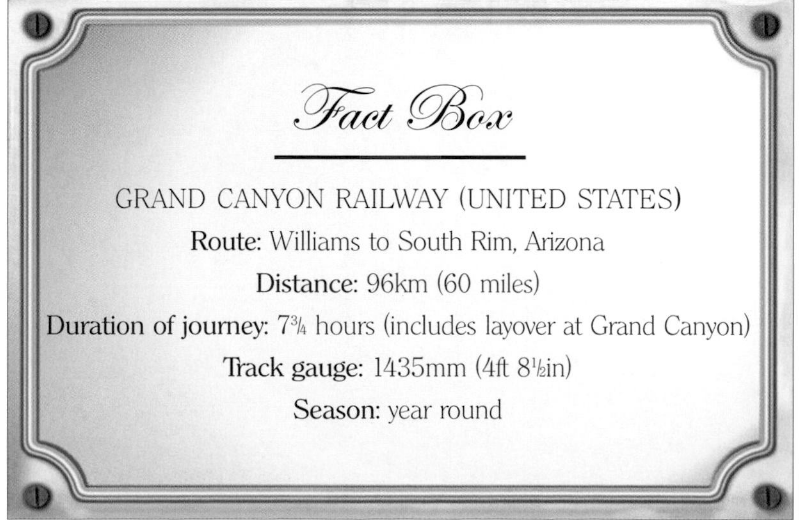

Fact Box

GRAND CANYON RAILWAY (UNITED STATES)

Route: Williams to South Rim, Arizona

Distance: 96km (60 miles)

Duration of journey: 7¾ hours (includes layover at Grand Canyon)

Track gauge: 1435mm (4ft 8½in)

Season: year round

STEAMTOWN NATIONAL HISTORIC SITE

Steve Barry

Says Phoebe Snow about to go
Upon a trip to Buffalo,
'My gown stays white from morn to night
Upon the Road of Anthracite.'

The Delaware, Lackawanna & Western Railroad billed itself as 'The Road of Anthracite', as the dense, clean-burning coal not only provided fuel for its steam locomotives but was also the commodity that furnished the bulk of its freight revenues. And Phoebe Snow, dressed in her gown of white, became the Lackawanna's symbol. Anthracite burned in the locomotive's firebox was not going to produce smoke and cinders to smudge her dress!

In the end, though, the anthracite deposits of northeastern Pennsylvania were depleted and other coal sources were found. Scranton, the city at the heart of the Lackawanna, saw its economy decline as the railroad struggled to survive. Ultimately, the Lackawanna became a part of the government-created Conrail in 1976, and much of its main line was downgraded or abandoned. But in 1984, a museum looking to

ABOVE *Closeup of the builder's plate of Canadian Pacific No. 2317, built in June 1923 by the Montreal Locomotive Works.*

RIGHT *Four locomotives rest at the former Lackawanna roundhouse in Scranton. No. 3713, at far right, is undergoing restoration.*

STEAMTOWN NATIONAL HISTORIC SITE, UNITED STATES

relocate from Vermont came knocking on Scranton's door and brought renewed life to the Route of Phoebe Snow. But more about this later.

Today, visitors to Scranton will find Steamtown National Historic Site occupying the former locomotive shop complex of the Lackawanna. The roundhouse has been meticulously restored, and the steam backshop continues to maintain and rebuild locomotives just as it did during the heyday of anthracite. A world-class railroad museum surrounds the turntable. And waiting at the station is a long train of former Lackawanna passenger coaches ready to head eastward up the steep grade into the Pocono Mountains.

Driving into Steamtown, visitors are first greeted by the sight of a small steam locomotive from the Raritan River Railroad in neighbouring New Jersey. A little further along is a massive locomotive from the Reading Company that formerly served the coalfields southwest of Scranton. An equally impressive locomotive from the Midwest, formerly operated by the Grand Trunk Western Railway, is next. And finally, next to the parking area, is an example of the largest steam locomotives ever constructed, a 'Big Boy' locomotive that served the Union Pacific in Wyoming and Utah in the western United States. This is truly a steam fan's paradise.

During the summer season, Steamtown offers one steam excursion a day each weekend. There are three possible destinations, and a complete schedule of which destination is offered on each weekend is available at the start of the season. One possible destination is Carbondale, Pennsylvania, heading north out of Scranton over trackage once owned by the Delaware & Hudson Railway. This route passes through some old coal-mining towns that have fallen upon hard times, and some industrial remnants of the coalfields can be observed from the train as well.

But the real treat is the trains that operate eastward out of Scranton over the old Lackawanna main line. Most trips terminate at Tobyhanna, Pennsylvania, some 48km (30 miles) from Scranton. During the autumn colours, excursions continue another 48km (30 miles) beyond Tobyhanna to the scenic Delaware Water Gap, a break in the Appalachian Mountains carved millions of years ago by the Delaware River. These are the trips that most tax the capabilities of Steamtown's locomotives.

Once passengers are settled into their seats, the train whistles off from the station and almost immediately begins to climb a stiff, steady grade. The steam trains share the station platform with electric streetcars of the Electric City Trolley Museum, which has restored service over part of the old Lackawanna & Wyoming Valley Railway ('The Laurel Line'). The impressive building visible on the left immediately after leaving Steamtown is the former passenger station and office building of the Lackawanna Railroad, now housing a hotel.

Perhaps you noticed the Lackawanna station is built out of concrete. As you ride along the main line, you'll notice a lot of other concrete rail structures. The concrete industry had a firm foothold in the areas southeast of Scranton, and the Lackawanna wasn't shy about using the stuff in its construction. The Lackawanna constructed buildings to last for decades and, because of its nearly indestructible nature, much of the Lackawanna's infrastructure has indeed survived the generations. North of

RIGHT *Canadian Pacific No. 2317 passes under a former Erie Railroad branch while riding the Lackawanna main line east of Scranton on its way to Moscow, Pennsylvania.*

2317
2317
2317
CANADIAN PACIFIC

Scranton, in the town of Nicholson, is the largest concrete railroad viaduct ever constructed. Just a few miles north of Nicholson, at Martins Creek, is another concrete viaduct. Steamtown used this line (which was the Lackawanna main line heading west) for several years, but now only freight trains ride across these magnificent bridges.

Through the open windows of the passenger coaches, the locomotive can be heard loudly working as it digs into the grade and enters Roaring Brook Gorge. Passengers are advised to close their windows for a minute or so, however, as the train briefly enters the darkness of Nay Aug Tunnel. Back into fresh air, the train continues to pass remnants of the past. The large used auto parts dealer visible on the left-hand side of the train is housed in the former Dunmore shops of the Erie Railroad, and two abandoned Erie branch lines bridge over the Lackawanna route you are riding.

Next up on the list of scenic highlights is Elmhurst Reservoir, a beautiful man-made lake that appears on the train's left side, and soon thereafter are the restored Lackawanna freight and passenger stations in the town of Moscow, which was the eastern end of regular Steamtown operations until 2002. The grade has lessened slightly, but it's still all uphill as the train passes the passenger station and signal tower at Gouldsboro. The lakes along the tracks through this area once provided ice for the Lackawanna's refrigerator cars – the cars used to haul perishable foods – before the era of mechanically refrigerated cars. Each winter, however, local townspeople still come out onto the lake with large saws to harvest the ice manually from the top of the lake – some of the ice is used for refrigeration, but mostly the ice-harvesting is done just to keep this historic practice alive. The ice is put into insulated sheds – ice that was harvested in February is still in the shed in June! Finally, the train arrives at Tobyhanna, where another Lackawanna station and signal tower stand.

For those fortunate enough to be taking the trip to the Delaware Water Gap, the adventure is only half over. Departing Tobyhanna, the train reaches the top of the grade after a mile or so, and at the town of Pocono Summit River (site of another Lackawanna station) the tracks begin to head downhill towards the Delaware. The train twists and turns as it descends the Pocono Mountains, passing a location aptly named Devil's Hole. As the train passes through the town of Cresco, those sitting on the left-hand side will see the restored depot, while those on the right will get a good view of the train on a big open curve. The train slows as it approaches the busy streets of East Stroudsburg, where the signal tower is being restored and the station has been converted to a restaurant. Yet another station, this one just in the beginning stages of restoration, is located at the town of Delaware Water Gap. It is at this point the train begins its journey along the Delaware River through one of the most spectacular (albeit short) canyons in the eastern United States.

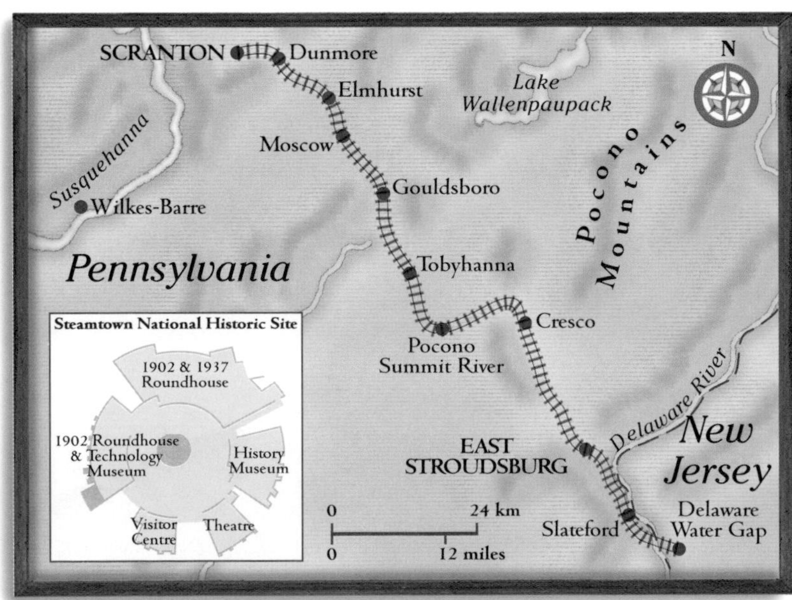

The tracks through the Water Gap see passenger service only on relatively rare occasions (although freight trains pass through here on a daily basis), so the train proceeds slowly, giving passengers an extraordinary view out of the left-hand side of the train. Cliffs soar high overhead, and the rushing Delaware River forms rapids in its rocky bed. The train passes right through the heart of the gap, finally emerging near the town of Slateford. The large concrete viaduct overhead carried the continuation of the Lackawanna main line as it headed for Hoboken, New Jersey, across the Hudson River from New York City. It is here, at Slateford, that the locomotives will run around to the opposite end of the train for the return trip to Scranton.

What is it that makes Steamtown National Historic Site so special? Apart from the outstanding train ride, it is one of the finest examples of steam-era infrastructure still standing in North America – and the buildings are still used for the purpose they were originally built, which is to maintain steam power. The turntable is still used daily as locomotives leave the roundhouse for the day's trip, and surrounding the table is one of the best railroad museums in the country. To appreciate fully what Steamtown is today, perhaps a quick look back at where it started can lend some perspective.

Fact Box

STEAMTOWN NATIONAL HISTORIC SITE (UNITED STATES)

Route: Scranton, Pennsylvania, to Slateford, New Jersey

Distance: 96km (60 miles)

Duration of journey: 3 hours to Tobyhanna; 7½ hours to Delaware Water Gap

Track gauge: 1435mm (4ft 8½in)

Season: late May to late October

ABOVE LEFT *On the steep grade out of Scranton, trains pass through Nay Aug Tunnel, making for plenty of noise from the hard-working locomotive.*

In the early 1960s steam power had just about vanished from the United States, and was running its final miles in Canada. F. Nelson Blount, a self-made millionaire, wanted to find a way to preserve steam for future generations. He envisioned a railroad that solely operated steam as the means to show future generations what railroading was like in the 1940s and 1950s. To make his vision come true, he began to purchase unused steam locomotives from all across the USA and Canada. After a few false starts, the collection finally found a home near Bellows Falls, Vermont, as Steamtown USA.

Work was underway on establishing the museum when Blount died in a light plane accident in 1968. Unfortunately, a custody battle ensued over the collection, with some pieces being shipped away. Those that remained came under the auspices of the Steamtown Foundation, which was perpetually underfunded.

In the early 1980s, Steamtown hired renowned rail writer and photographer Don Ball, Jr., as its manager. Under Ball's leadership, the equipment was cosmetically restored and the grounds were given a makeover. Ball knew, however, that the limited tourism dollars available in Vermont would not be enough and he sought a metropolitan location where the collection could be accessed by a large population.

Meanwhile, Scranton was feeling the effects of the decline in Pennsylvania's rail and coal industries. The city acquired the former Lackawanna roundhouse, shop buildings and yard, providing Steamtown with a new home less than two hours away from the major population centres of New York City and Philadelphia. In 1983 Steamtown bade farewell to Vermont and moved south.

Times remained tough, however, as neither the city nor the museum had a lot of money to spend, and the picture was further clouded by Ball's untimely death. In the late 1980s the state of Pennsylvania got into the act and Steamtown became a unit of the National Park Service. Some $60 million was poured into the Steamtown project, and in 1995 Steamtown National Historic Site opened its doors.

What can a visitor see at Steamtown? By all means, a visit to the roundhouse is in order. Historically, the roundhouse was the place where locomotives were brought between runs for light maintenance, and the Steamtown roundhouse still performs this function. You can watch a locomotive being readied for the day from the gallery that has been constructed inside along the building's perimeter. You can go outside the roundhouse as the locomotive backs onto the turntable and is lined up for the track that will take it out to its train.

Beyond the roundhouse is the workshop where the Lackawanna performed heavy repairs. Today, as many as four steam locomotives can be found in the workshop in various stages of rebuilding. It's amazing to see how far a locomotive has to be torn down before it can be put back into service. Rangers are on hand to explain to visitors what they are looking at – and depending on the level of the shop work that needs to be performed, some of what is seen needs a lot of explanation!

If you have wondered what the inside of a steam locomotive looks like, you'll find the answer in the museum, where a full-size locomotive has been cut away to reveal its inner workings. Also in the museum are displays on rail history around Scranton, and interpretive areas on the people who worked on the railroads. You'll probably need a couple of hours to explore all there is to see in the museum.

For anyone interested in finding out more about steam railroading – not just how the mighty locomotives pulled passenger trains, but how railroads affected the people and industries of the areas they served – then Steamtown will likely answer a lot of your questions. While many museums will interpret steam in terms of a ride, Steamtown will show you that the ride is only part of what steam railroading was all about.

MOUNT WASHINGTON COG RAILWAY

Steve Barry

HAVE YOU EVER WONDERED WHAT IT WOULD BE LIKE TO RIDE A STEAM TRAIN that went so high you could almost touch the sky? That's what it's like to ride the Mount Washington Cog Railway, which ascends the highest mountain in the northeastern United States.

Mount Washington is located in the Presidential Range of the White Mountains of New Hampshire. Surrounded by tall mountains such as Mounts Jefferson, Adams and Madison (named for past US presidents), Mount Washington is a giant among giants, rising 1916.5m (6288ft) into the sky. It is up the flank of this behemoth that tiny trains make their climb to the summit.

A journey on the Mount Washington Cog Railway begins at the Marshfield Station, located near the historic resort of Bretton Woods, New Hampshire. Adjacent to the station is the railroad's maintenance complex, where seven nearly identical steam locomotives are cared for. The locomotives, built in the 1890s, have been extensively overhauled and rebuilt over the years so that very little material remains from the original construction. Only locomotive No. 1, named *Mount Washington*, is intact from 1890, but it no longer sees service.

ABOVE *With the steepest portion of the climb behind it, a Mount Washington Cog train rounds the final curve for its ascent to the summit.*

RIGHT *Two downhill trains wait in the siding at Skyline Switch near the summit of Mount Washington to allow an uphill train to pass.*

MOUNT WASHINGTON COG RAILWAY, UNITED STATES

A closer look at these locomotives reveals many unique features. Unlike regular steam locomotives, which have one set of cylinders on each side, these have two cylinders on each side pointed in opposite directions. And while conventional locomotives have rods connecting the pistons within the cylinders to the wheels, the rods extending from these cylinders seem to connect to nothing. A closer inspection reveals that the rods are actually connected to two axles, and each axle has a cog wheel mounted under the centre of the locomotive that engages the rack rail, which is itself toothed to engage the cog wheel, running between the regular rails on the track. And the boilers of the locomotives are not parallel to the ground, but are tilted forward at a sharp angle. This arrangement ensures that the boiler (and the water inside) will always remain level even though the locomotive is always running up a steep grade.

Looking around the grounds of the station, you can't help but notice a locomotive with an upright boiler on display. This locomotive is named *Peppersass* (because it looks like a pepper sauce bottle) and was the first locomotive to ascend Mount Washington, on 3 July 1869. The locomotive was retired when the 'modern' fleet of the 1890s was built, but it was brought out of retirement in 1929 for one last run up the mountain. But perhaps we should save the story of the final run of *Peppersass* until we get back from our ride.

Mount Washington dominates the surrounding countryside, and even generates its own weather. Smart travellers should plan on spending several days in the area (and there is plenty to do, including several other steam and diesel tourist train rides within comfortable driving distance) until they get that perfect day when the summit is clear. These conditions occur only about six or seven times a month, so patience will pay off. But once that clear day arrives, get down to the station and get your ticket because the trains will fill up quickly.

After purchasing your ticket and getting the 'All aboard' from the conductor, choose a seat that will allow you to look out of the left side as the train heads uphill. The seats are not plush, but this isn't a luxury trip – it's an experience. Once everybody is on board, the conductor will give the all-clear and the locomotive will begin to push a single coach up the hill (each locomotive can push one coach – if ridership demands additional capacity, a second complete train of one engine and coach is dispatched). After crossing the Ammonoosuc River, the grade begins immediately and passengers are pushed back into their seats as the coach rises up the hill.

This trip won't set any speed records as, working as hard as it can, the locomotive will attain a speed of only about five miles an hour. This initial climb is known as Cold Spring Hill, and it takes about 15 minutes for the train to crest the grade at an elevation of 1158m (3800ft) and come to a stop at the Waumbek water tank where the already thirsty locomotive will have its tender refilled. During the trip the locomotive consumes 3785 litres (1000 gallons) of water and burns one ton of coal (all of it shovelled by hand into the firebox by the hard-working fireman). After taking on water (and possibly meeting a downhill train) the ride continues, with the beautiful Ammonoosuc Ravine off to the left.

LEFT *Midway through its journey, an uphill train passes the appropriately named Halfway House. Marshfield Base Station, the train's departure point, can be seen in the distance.*

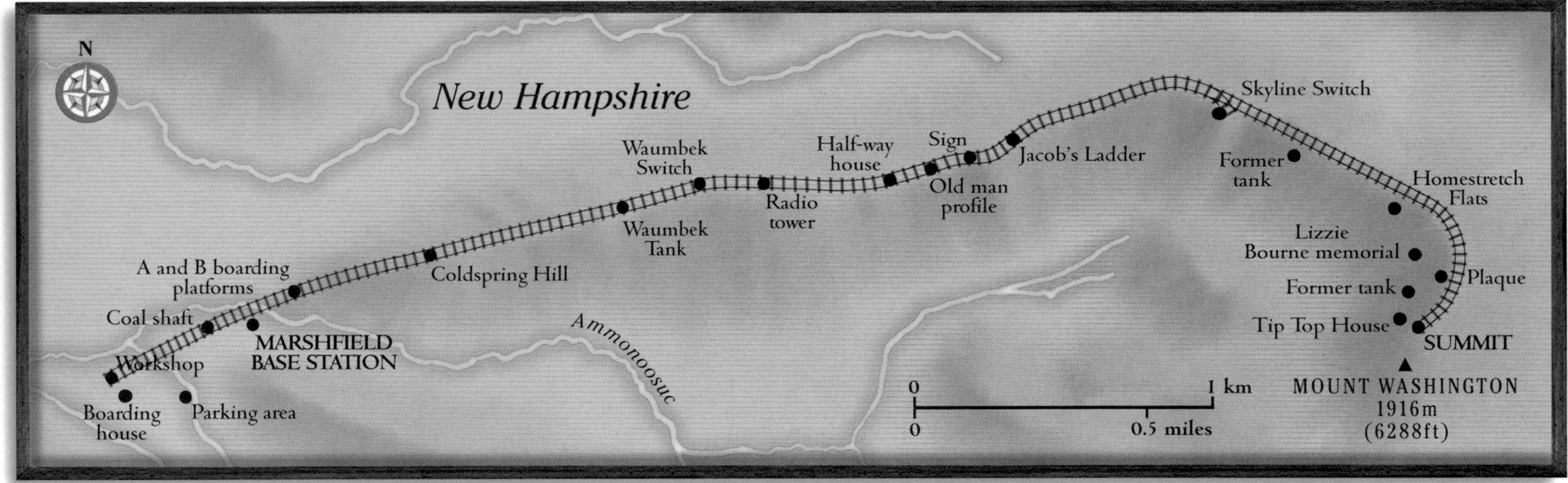

The air becomes cooler and the trees sparser as the train continues its uphill assault. The Halfway House, a red building on the right, marks the 1463m (4800ft) mark of the climb. Soon the trees are left behind, replaced by low brush and exposed rocks. Next comes the steepest part of the trip, a curving trestle that is 91.5m (300ft) in length. Known as Jacob's Ladder, this is on a 37.41 per cent grade (the train rises 37 feet for every 100 feet it moves forward). To put it in perspective, the people sitting at the front of the coach are 4m (14ft) higher than the folks at the back!

Once the climb up Jacob's Ladder is complete, the next highlight is Long Trestle. Not as steep and twisting as Jacob's Ladder, it is still the second steepest part of the railroad. After cresting this hill, the train arrives at Skyline Switch, a passing siding where the uphill train may meet a train coming down. The elevation is now 1707m (5600ft), and the view from here is breathtaking. The Great Gulf spreads down and away, and impressive views of Mts. Adams, Clay and Madison can be seen. Looking up, the summit of Mount Washington is visible, albeit still nearly 213m (700ft) higher. If two trains meet at Skyline Switch, the conductor must throw a switch involving nine moveable pieces to change tracks so that one train can enter the siding. The main line to the summit once boasted three of these complex track junctions, but two – at the base station and at Waumbek Tank – have been replaced with mechanical switches that require only the push of a button to change tracks. Skyline Siding is due to be replaced by a siding at the summit, eliminating the last of the old manual switches.

Finally the train arrives at the summit, where some of the world's strongest wind speeds have been recorded. On the clearest days you can see Maine and Vermont, and even a glimpse of the Atlantic Ocean. The train will remain at the summit for about 20 minutes, and passengers can either reboard the same train for the ride down or ride a later train. There is an observatory at the summit (with a museum), as well as a weather station. Tip Top House, built in 1853, is also here. Part of the original group of stone buildings built at the summit, it is today the only survivor.

While touring the museum, pause to reflect on the history of the railroad and the exploration of Mount Washington. Sylvester Marsh climbed the mountain in 1857 (115 years after Darby Field made the first ascent) and, after losing his way near the summit, determined that there had to be a better way to reach the top. He began working on the design of the world's first cog railway, but when he presented his idea to the New Hampshire legislature they declared with disdain that he 'might as well build a railway to the moon'. Nonetheless, since Marsh had merely requested a charter (and not money) his request was granted. On August 29, 1866, *Peppersass* made a successful test run over the first completed section of track. It became apparent the railroad was more than a wild dream, and stockholders soon signed up. Construction of the line began, and the railroad reached the future site of Waumbek Tank in 1867 and Jacob's Ladder a year later. On 3 July 1869, *Peppersass* reached the summit.

While one might think the downhill trip would be much quicker than the uphill run, it is only slightly shorter. The locomotive actually coasts down the mountain, using compressed air in the cylinders to control its speed. While the locomotive is capable of easing itself downhill, it cannot hold itself and a loaded coach on the grade. The train's conductor becomes the brakeman for the downhill run and stands next to two brake wheels mounted to the downhill end of the coach. His job is to make sure the coach only gently touches the locomotive during the downhill trip. Perhaps this is a good time to mention that the locomotive and coach are not coupled – gravity keeps them united. With the brakeman constantly adjusting the drag to the coach, the train eases back down to the bottom. Finally, the train arrives back at Marshfield Station.

About the last run of *Peppersass*: when it was brought out of retirement in 1929 and made its return to the summit, it did not fare well on the downhill trip. It ran away and crashed. Aren't you glad you didn't know this until your trip was safely finished?

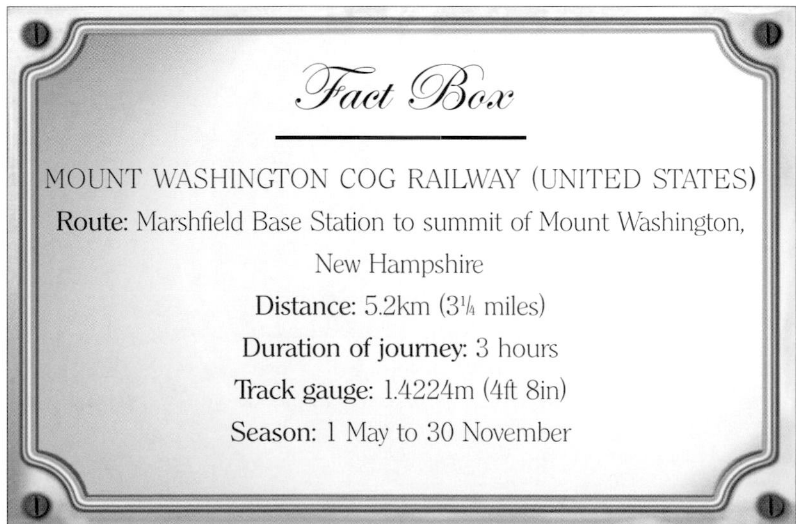
Fact Box

MOUNT WASHINGTON COG RAILWAY (UNITED STATES)

Route: Marshfield Base Station to summit of Mount Washington, New Hampshire

Distance: 5.2km (3¼ miles)

Duration of journey: 3 hours

Track gauge: 1.4224m (4ft 8in)

Season: 1 May to 30 November

Ecuador

STEAM ON THE DEVIL'S NOSE

John Parker

LOCOMOTIVE NO. 53 STANDS NEXT TO THE DERELICT BUILDING that was once Sibambe station, enveloped by the sounds and smells of steam – the incessant chatter of the air brake, the ominous rumble of an oil burner at rest, the sizzle of water dripping on hot metal. She faces one of the most famous and fearsome railway journeys in the world. The train is a motley collection of wagons and carriages. The crew are eager but acutely aware of the struggle ahead. But how did it get here? Where did it come from? Does it have a future? The answers to these and many other questions lie in a timeless battle to tame a wild landscape.

The history of Ecuador's railway, its day-to-day struggles and its future are all inexorably linked to geography. Warm tropical beaches, fertile rainforests and snowcapped volcanoes are all found within a country that is little bigger than New Zealand. Into this geographical cauldron must be added the unpredictable equatorial climate, with El Niño a periodic and devastating visitor. Ecuadorians are tough and resourceful people – but then, they need to be.

ABOVE *Locomotive No. 44 works hard as it approaches the second zigzag on the Devil's Nose. The two zigzags, together with gradients as steep as 1 in 18, take the line 200m (600ft) up and over the Devil's Nose.*

RIGHT *This bird's-eye view of the Devil's Nose makes plain the fearsome challenge faced by railway builders in this part of the Andes. Sibambe station is visible at the lower left of the photo.*

The ancient civilizations of the Andes found enormous treasure buried in the mountains. Gold, silver and precious stones created the wealthy Inca empire but also attracted the interest of the Spanish conquistadors. Spanish colonization was total and bloody, but by the middle of the 19th century Ecuador had won its independence. Like most young nations, it had a pressing need to improve transportation, and discussions began about the possibility of building Ecuador's first railway. Guayaquil and Quito, the two largest cities, presented an obvious first choice for a rail link, which would reduce the seven-day journey by mule to around 24 hours. However, although only a little over 450km (275 miles) apart, the two cities are separated by the fearsome obstacle of the Andes Mountains.

In theory, the line could have run northwards along the coastal strip and then turned eastward over the Andes to reach Quito, but this route presented the railway with the problems both of crossing a predominantly wet area and surmounting impossible gradients. The early engineers were left with no choice other than to build a 1065mm (3ft 6in) narrow gauge railway through the 'Avenue of the Volcanoes', one of the most geologically unstable areas on earth. Volcanoes can, and do, erupt on a regular basis, covering vast areas in ash. The inhabitants of Quito don't have to dream of a white Christmas – many mornings of the year they wake up to one!

At first, progress was slow and the line from Guayaquil did not reach Milagro until 1874. A further 20 years elapsed before the American engineers, Archer Harman and Edward Morely, began construction of the section northwards through Bucay and on towards Quito. They were faced with the task of surmounting nearly 160km (100 miles) of mountains with a 4000m (12,000ft) summit and an average height of well over 2500m (8000ft). But things got worse. Within 80km (50 miles) they came up against a fearful perpendicular rock face, known the world over as El Nariz del Diablo – the Devil's Nose. They had already achieved an engineering miracle, but this would require divine intervention.

In the end the solution was simple but awe-inspiring. The line zigzags through two reverses and takes nearly 3.25km (2 miles) to rise some 200m (600ft) to the top – most of it at a gradient of 1 in 18. The journey on the 3m (10ft) wide ledge cut into the mountainside gives first-time visitors a hair-raising experience as they begin the death-defying climb from the valley floor at Sibambe towards the summit of 'the nose'.

The line is remarkably busy, as the state railway company ENFE (Empresa Nacional de Ferrocarriles del Estado) has already grasped the value of this most amazing tourist attraction. Most days of the week an *autoferro* (a motor coach with railway wheels) winds its way from Alausi to Sibambe. In typical Ecuadorian fashion, the roof is packed with daredevil riders who show no fear as the *autoferro* bumbles

ABOVE *A cloud of smoke hangs in the mountain air as an ENFE train negotiates a narrow valley. The locomotives used on the Guayaquil–Quito railway are oil-burning and so produce considerable quantities of smoke.*

its way along the trackbed some 2m (6ft) away from a 100m (300ft) precipice! The track ahead shows a disconcerting lack of uniformity. Sleepers are missing, the gauge is often nominal and the railway fights a constant battle against rock falls and erosion. In some sort of drunken union, track and train bounce up and down with just enough shuddering and juddering to suggest that you might go over the edge at any time! But you don't, and for all these dangers it is like no other railway journey in the world. The perfect white-knuckle ride!

It is, of course, some time since steam saw regular service over 'the nose', but a recent surge of interest in the railway has brought the possibility of a steam revival. There is a new political will to return the line to regular use, and even talk of reopening the line to regular through traffic. Slowly but surely, ENFE is collecting the rolling stock necessary to run steam on a regular basis. They now have three serviceable locomotives: a 2-6-0 No. 11 and a pair of 2-8-0s (Nos. 17 & 53). All are of American origin – built in Philadelphia by Baldwin in 1900, 1935 and 1953, respectively – and re-create perfectly the feel of a bygone era. Add to these, two exquisite passenger cars and a selection of freight wagons and the scene is set fair for a steam revival.

The Minister of Tourism is now involved, and the media is taking a real interest in recent developments. This is good news as the railway holds a special place in the affection of all Ecuadorians. Its integration into the fabric of daily life is a fascinating story in its own right. The Latin temperament has no place for a stony-faced and impersonal transport system, so once Guayaquil and Quito were linked, the railway became enmeshed in the day-to-day routine of every town and village along its route. Buildings grew up around the newly built iron road. People and their goods came and went. Livestock was as common a passenger as any man, woman or child. The track itself seemed to become the focal point of existence: children played on it, animals ran alongside it and barked or squawked at the monstrously noisy visitors. The railway brought trade and it brought adventure – but, above all, it brought life.

Little has changed now that the railway is being revived. What better place is there, after all, for someone to erect a market stall than on the relatively solid foundation provided at no expense by those thoughtful people who run the railway? Most towns have a weekly market, and it is a truly amazing sight to watch the train move in slow procession through its very heart. Progress is slow, as dozens of people run around removing their wares from the path of the locomotive. The engine driver makes furious sounds with both the whistle and the large brass bell that sits astride the boiler. The noise is deafening, but to no avail. There is a natural pace about this encounter that will not be changed by a show of exasperated impatience.

ABOVE *With its carriages poised at vertigo-inducing angles, locomotive No. 44 hauls a train up the second zigzag on the Devil's Nose. Variations in gauge, hand-operated braking and the threat of landslides are just some of the hazards of travel on this line.*

People around here do things at their own speed, and when it suits them. Besides which, the train is an interloper, disturbing the hustle and bustle of people making money... or talking... or sleeping... or just sitting around watching life drift by! After the train has passed, the stalls, the bric-a-brac, the ephemera of life are moved back to their rightful and God-given place. The people return to whatever they were doing. The invader has been driven out of town. The animals soon lose interest. Children begin to play again. There will be a repeat performance *mañana* (tomorrow) or – if the train somehow gets lost, or breaks down – 'the day after *mañana*'!

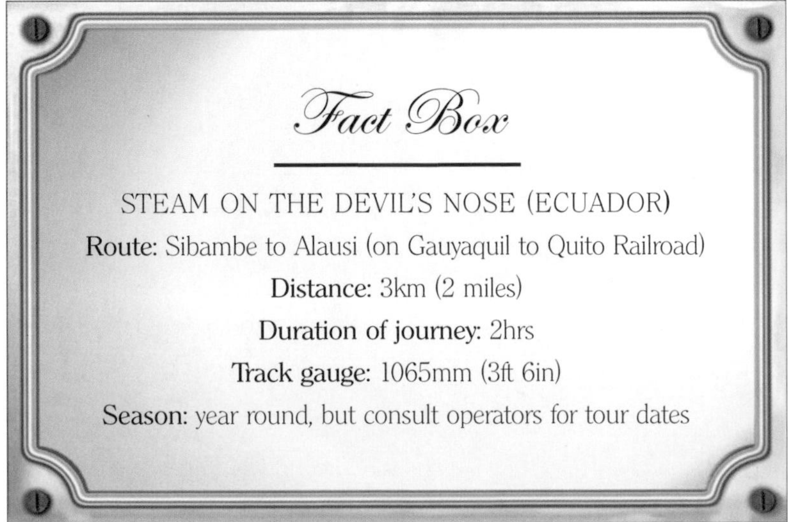

Fact Box

STEAM ON THE DEVIL'S NOSE (ECUADOR)

Route: Sibambe to Alausi (on Gauyaquil to Quito Railroad)

Distance: 3km (2 miles)

Duration of journey: 2hrs

Track gauge: 1065mm (3ft 6in)

Season: year round, but consult operators for tour dates

No railway can function without the men and women who dedicate their life to its operation, and Ecuador is no different. Steam may be exciting and different, but the hard, demanding and dirty work undertaken by the locomotive crews and the track gangs must never be forgotten. Ecuadorian locomotives were built to do the job of hauling trains. Few concessions were made to crew comfort or safety.

All the surviving locomotives are oil-fired and have that unique, low-pitched roaring sound so different from their coal-fired brethren. The locomotive footplate is not a place for the faint-hearted. It is noisy and dirty and, above all, incredibly dangerous. The oil burner gives out a great amount of heat, but in doing so breathes naked flames around the feet of anyone brave (or foolish) enough to stand nearby. There seems to be no set number of crew but, generally speaking, the driver and firemen tackle the difficult job of driving this swaying monster, whilst their colleagues ride 'shotgun' on the tender. Most Ecuadorian men have an intensely macho attitude to the world in general and towards other men in particular. It is not in their nature to show any sign of fear. With frightening bravado they stand and combat the forces of gravity and the violent movement beneath their feet. But this is nothing compared with the bravery shown by *los brequeros* – the brakemen. Most Ecuadorian locomotives simply do not have enough braking power to deal with the ferocious gradients they encounter, so every freight wagon and every passenger coach carries upon its roof a hand-operated braking system, actuated by a large spoked wheel. Each wheel is under the control of a brakeman. It is his job to help the driver and firemen descend safely, but as if this isn't dangerous enough they insist on walking the entire length of the coach on a walkway only 60cm (2ft) wide but around 4m (13ft) above the ground!

OPPOSITE *With fearless* brequeros *clustered atop the freight wagons, a Guayaquil–Quito train crosses a viaduct amid splendid Andean scenery.*

RIGHT *No. 17, a 2-8-0 built by Baldwin in 1935, is one of the few steam locomotives that still makes the run over the Devil's Nose.*

Derailments are common, but the crews treat them with disdain. As if by magic, they produce jacks, levers and assorted equipment, and the ritual begins. A noisy huddle forms around the loco, cigarettes are lit and animated debate ensues about the best way to proceed. Brave souls disappear under the locomotive, instructions are shouted out and the driving wheels spin as the driver opens the regulator. Within a few seconds, the job is done. Knowledge is valuable but experience is priceless!

Sibambe station is a forlorn monument to a prosperous past. The shops have gone, the tiny church is derelict. Once serving a busy junction, the station building is now just an empty shell, the roof gone to provide shelter to more needy souls. No longer do trains from Guayaquil or Quito jostle for space with those that descended into the valley from the Cuenca branch. The branch is no more and through trains are all gone, the victim of a half-mile-long landslip at Chanchan. But where there is life, there is hope! Steam has returned to the Devil's Nose.

Locomotive No. 53 stands at the head of its train. The crew are ready. Train orders are given. The ride of a lifetime is about to begin. The gradient starts almost immediately and it's not long before the boiler pressure begins to fall. Cue the fireman, who turns a knob, releasing an enormous cloud of black smoke from the chimney. Nature has met its match. The 'Avenue of the Volcanoes' has competition. Steam builds up, the pace increases, the iron horse will not be beaten.

It is already halfway to the first reverse and the scenery is even more breathtaking. Sheer cliffs rise a thousand feet on both sides, and 'the nose' itself towers above the train. There is much work still to do. The loco slips, slips again, and begins to slow down. Sand is needed – and quickly! Two of the crew jump off the tender, run in front of the train and begin to sand the rails. They have no tools other than empty cocoa tins. The sand begins to work, and the locomotive's wheels begin to bite. The sanding crew seem reluctant to stop their labours, and climb onto the cowcatcher to continue. We arrive at the first reverse and after the briefest of pauses are off again – backwards! Nothing must stop us now, and the train makes maximum smoke, maximum effort and maximum noise. Above us the last part of the climb is just visible, below us a 100m (300ft) plunge into oblivion. The second reverse brings a brief respite before we tackle the last section. The gradient is fierce, the wheels squeal but victory is within our grasp. There is another bout of frenzied activity from the cocoa tins up front. Progress is steady. The sound of the locomotive echoes from the mountains. We have done it, we have taken steam over El Nariz del Diablo!

What of the future? There are now plans to use steam on a reasonably permanent basis. The line is more or less open to Quito, and the section from Sibambe to the summit at Urbina is a series of spectacular landscapes, with Mount Chimborazo an awe-inspiring backdrop. Much work has been done to improve the track and plans are afoot to franchise a steam operating concession. No doubt tour operators will be keen to capitalize on this most incredible railway once ENFE finalizes its planning. There is hope, and the promise of things to come. Steam is alive in Ecuador – just!

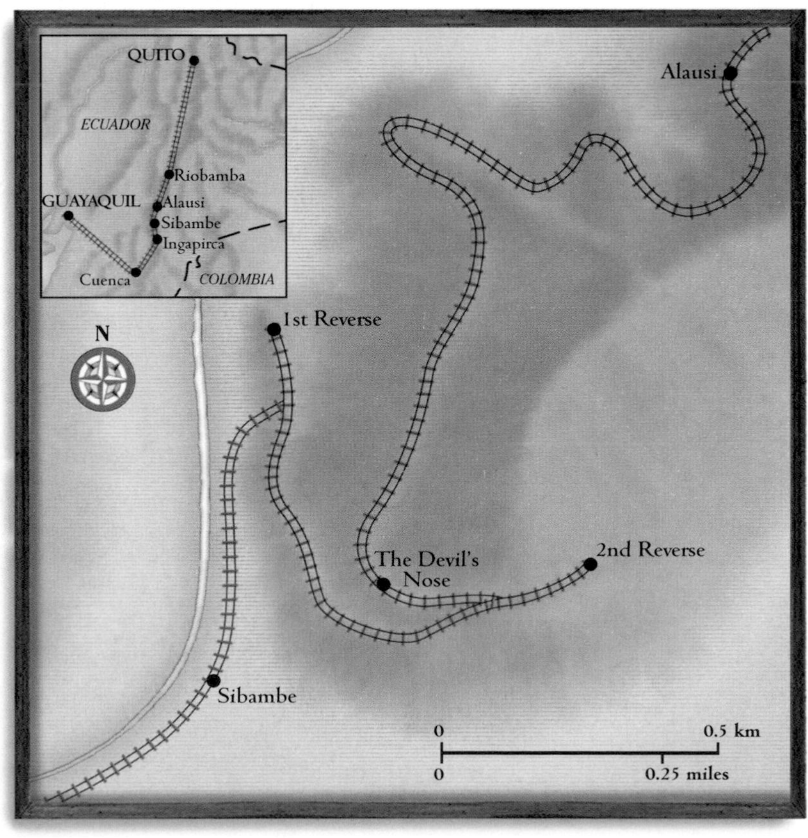

Argentina

THE OLD PATAGONIA EXPRESS

Carl G. Perelman

THE VAST, THINLY POPULATED REGION OF PATAGONIA lies in southern Argentina, where the Andes mountains straddle the border with Chile. Along the stark, treeless eastern rim of the mountains a special narrow gauge railway connects the towns of Jacobacci, El Maiten and Esquel. The 750mm (2ft 5½in) gauge railway is filled with history, having being conceived by Argentina's government as a means to open Patagonia to agricultural development. It was in 1908 that a minister in the Argentine goverment, Ezequiel Mejia Branches, proposed the construction of a rail line to kick-start the economy in the region. World War I and subsequent economic and political crises delayed construction. Finally, in 1945 the entire 402km (261-mile) route was opened, connecting Jacobacci and Esquel. The line included 646 curves, one tunnel and numerous bridges.

Over the years the railway has acquired the nickname La Trochita (Spanish for 'narrow gauge train'). It is otherwise known as the Old Patagonia Express to English-speaking railway enthusiasts. Due to the country's mounting economic difficulties, the Argentine government cancelled all services in 1993. However, the provinces of Chubut and Rio Negro saw the value of the train service, both as a basic mode of

ABOVE *A number plate bears the name of one of the six large companies created in 1948 when Argentina's railways were amalgamated. General Roca is the capital of Rio Negro province.*

RIGHT *After departing El Maiten, a southbound train chugs round one of the line's many curves. As the train passes through Ing Thomas the majestic Andes mountains are in view.*

ABOVE *Hauled by a Henschel 2-8-2 No. 114, the Old Patagonia Express departs from Esquel on the return journey to El Maiten.*

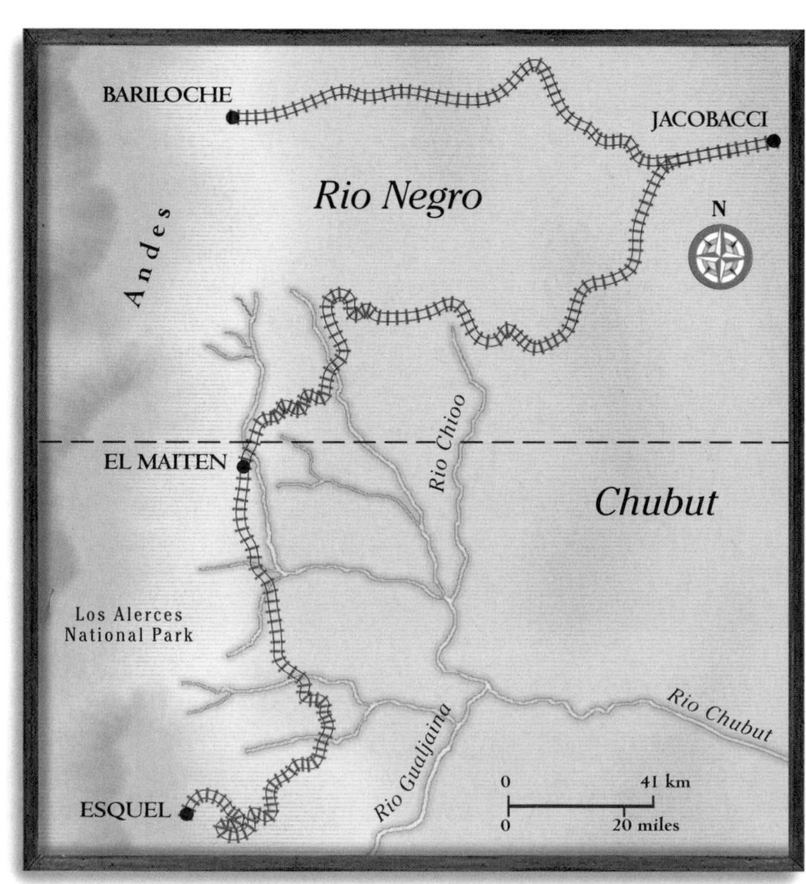

transport for locals and as a way of attracting tourists. However, in 1995 Rio Negro province decided to end its support, and services were discontinued between Jacobacci and El Maiten. Fortunately, Chubut kept its coffers open, allowing trains to operate between El Maiten and Esquel. In 2001 service was suspended between El Maiten and Esquel due to a damaged bridge, but trains were running again by 2003. No trains have operated on the northern leg of the railway for several years, but in 2002 Rio Negro's government declared both the yard and locomotive facility at Jacobacci a national historic monument, and thus in need of preservation. So it is possible that train services will soon resume on the dormant segment of the railway.

El Maiten is a town of 3500 people about an hour's drive from the mountainside tourist village of Bariloche. In the centre of town is the station, once a hive of activity. Just south of the station is the large railway yard and engine terminal. A stroll though the terminal finds numerous rusting freight cars and locomotives.

Each Wednesday the Old Patagonia Express departs El Maiten for the trip to Esquel, returning the following day. The railway is virtually the last such operation in South America to be powered exclusively by steam. The railway rosters 22 locomotives, constructed by Baldwin in Philadelphia and by Henschel in Kassel, Germany. Most of these locomotives are configured in the 2-8-2 wheel arrangement, but only half a dozen remain in service. The railway uses waste oil to power these locomotives. Behind the locomotive runs a string of stark, wooden coaches, constructed several decades ago in Belgium. Wood-burning heaters provide warmth on cold mornings.

As the whistle blows, the train departs the station (kilometre 237). (Distances are still measured from the station at Jacobacci, which represents kilometre 0.) Picking up speed, it passes several farms. The engineer sounds the whistle ahead of the few dirt roads that cross the tracks. Soon, the train enters a stark, arid landscape, virtually devoid of trees. The majestic Andes mountains loom to the west.

A ride on the Patagonia Express is an experience for any rail fan. The sound of the steam locomotive and smell of the oil-laden smoke are reminders of railways of yesteryear. Travellers require a degree of hardiness, though, for unlike European trains there are no reclining seats or air conditioning. Section (unwelded) rail makes for a bumpy ride, and dust swirls through the train. However, a delicious slice of chocolate cake, purchased in the dining car, will satisfy even the hungriest traveller.

Soon the train arrives at Leleque (kilometre 287.3), a welcome oasis in this otherwise barren area. Tall trees surround both the railway and neighbouring huts, and friendly villagers come out to meet the train. The locomotive's hungry tender is in need of replenishment. A water column soon appears and the train comes to a halt. The fireman climbs out of the cab and positions the water spout to refill the tender.

At Lepa (kilometre 310.2), the train stops again for water, while sheep graze the right-of-way. The next town en route is Nahuel Pan (kilometre 383), where the thirsty locomotive takes on more water. The town is home to indigenous Mapuche Indians, and several stores near the station sell Mapuche crafts and clothing to visiting tourists.

Upon departing Nahuel Pan, the train twists and turns through the foothills of the Andes, and eventually starts its long descent into Esquel. Mountain goats can be seen foraging near the track. Suddenly, the town comes into view, and the train pulls into Esquel station (kilometre 402). Passengers disembark and the locomotive is detached from the train, chugging towards an old-fashioned turntable. Watched by curious children, workers use muscle power to move the turntable through 180 degrees to spin the locomotive around. The locomotive then heads toward the shed to be put to rest for the night.

Esquel is not just another small town, and has more to see than just the railway. It is a mecca for tourism, being located near the large Los Alerces National Park, which offers spectacular vistas of the Andes, as well as camping and sightseeing. For those not wishing to brave the outdoors, Esquel has several hotels and fine dining. During the southern hemisphere summer (December–March), a steam-hauled tourist train operates daily – except Thursday and Sunday – to Nahuel Pan and back.

After an overnight stay in Esquel, it's time to return to El Maiten on board the train, which departs with a toot of the whistle. Sitting back, the traveller can daydream of the days before fast electric trains and diesel propulsion. However, this is not a dream, but a reality. Travel on the Patagonia Express is an experience to be savoured.

ABOVE *Curious locals mill around the station as an early-morning passenger train takes on water at Nahuel Pan.*

Fact Box

THE OLD PATAGONIA EXPRESS (ARGENTINA)

Route: El Maiten to Esquel, Chubut province

Distance: 165km (102 miles)

Duration of journey: 2 days (includes overnight stop in Esquel)

Track gauge: 750mm (2½ft)

Season: weekly throughout the year (departures from El Maiten on Wednesdays)

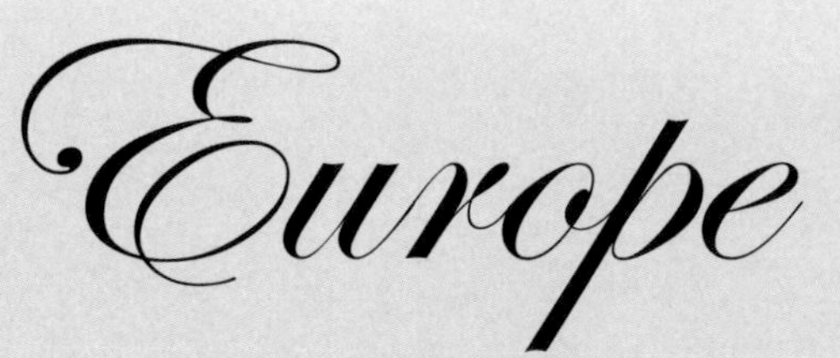
Europe

Pm 36-2

United Kingdom

FFESTINIOG RAILWAY

Anthony Lambert

IF ASKED TO FIND ONE OF THE MOST SCENICALLY DRAMATIC PLACES in Britain for a tourist railway, you would be hard put to find somewhere better than the mountains of Snowdonia, in northern Wales. Yet the origins of the Ffestiniog Railway lie not in tourism but in the popularity of slate as a roofing material. It was to move slate extracted from the quarries around Blaenau Ffestiniog that the Festiniog Railway (FR) came into being (using an anglicized version of the Welsh name).

The 20km (13½-mile) Festiniog Railway was built to supplant the packhorses formerly used to take the slate to the coast. It was promoted and built between Blaenau Ffestiniog and Port Madoc using the same track gauge as the tramways at the quarry – 597mm (1ft 11½in). The harbour at Port Madoc was the indirect result of an unemployment relief scheme carried out by the area's principal landowner, William Madocks, the MP for Boston in Lincolnshire. In 1811 he built an embankment known as the Cob across the mouth of the Glaslyn estuary, reclaiming thousands of acres of land from the sea but so altering the currents that they scoured an ideal harbour for ships. It was named Port Madoc, nicely commemorating both its founder and the legendary Prince Madog, said to have sailed to the New World from this spot in the 12th century.

ABOVE *The maker's plate of No. 10* Merddin Emrys *shows the date the locomotive was produced by the Ffestiniog Railway's Boston Lodge works.*

RIGHT *Pulling a train of slate wagons as it was built to do in 1863, 0–4–0STT Palmerston climbs the spiral at Dduallt while sister locomotive Prince stands in the station.*

PREVIOUS PAGES *A Polish Ol49 2-6-2, hauling a scheduled passenger service near Adamowo, takes a curve at speed.*

By incorporating some impressive stone embankments and two tunnels, the builders of the Festiniog Railway achieved a relatively easy maximum gradient of 1 in 80; this was necessary to allow horses to pull the empty slate wagons up from the coast and ride down the hill in 'dandy' wagons on the loaded, gravity-operated slate trains. Today, the railway operates gravity trains of dozens of slate wagons on special days to show visitors the original mode of operation.

The railway opened in 1836, but began to attract international attention in 1863 when steam traction was introduced – the first time that steam had been applied to so small a gauge anywhere in the world. Two locomotives built by George England & Co. of London were delivered in 1863, and two more the following year when permission was granted by the Board of Trade for the FR to run passenger trains – another first for a narrow gauge line in Britain. To keep the passengers' weight as central as possible, back-to-back seats ran the length of the carriages. Some of these early four-wheel vehicles survive in the FR's collection of historic coaches.

The FR was soon handling over 50,000 tons of slate a year, and needed a way to increase capacity. Doubling the line was considered, but a cheaper solution was found in a new type of powerful locomotive that would again draw the eyes of the international engineering fraternity – and a visit by envoys of the Russian Tsar. Designed by Robert Fairlie, the Double Fairlie looks like two locomotives joined back-to-back, but in fact has a single long boiler and firebox. What was equally revolutionary was the use of two swivelling bogies, each with a pair of cylinders to power the driving wheels. (A comparable layout is used on modern diesel and electric locomotives.) The concept of articulated steam locomotives led to tremendous export orders for British locomotive manufacturers.

So it was a portentous day in 1870 when a crowd of engineers, including Count Bobrinsky, who headed the Imperial Russian Commission, assembled to see what this new type of locomotive could do. It proved more than twice as powerful as the FR's other locomotives, and more Fairlies followed, including a single Fairlie named *Taliesin*, after the legendary Welsh bard. A re-creation of this locomotive, using a handful of original components, entered service in 1999, joining the three Double Fairlies which haul the FR's heaviest trains.

The FR claimed a third 'first' in 1873 when the first true bogie carriages in Britain entered service. These had iron frames, which was unusual for the time, most carriages being built almost entirely of wood. The railway has an enviable collection of historic carriages, with 17 dating from the 19th century and a set of five of the original four-wheel carriages of 1863–4 with the knifeboard (central) seats, nicknamed 'bug boxes'. These are used only on special gala days, sometimes hauled by one of the FR's first locomotives, *Prince*, which also dates from 1863-4. Few railways anywhere in the world can boast a working steam locomotive and carriages dating from the 1860s!

Most trains on the FR are hauled either by a Fairlie or by one of the tender-tank locomotives rescued from the Penrhyn Quarry Railway – another Welsh slate railway – and they leave from the picturesque station at Porthmadog Harbour. As soon as the train has left the sharply curved platform, it crosses Madocks' dead-straight Cob, with waves lapping one side and one of the best views of Snowdonia across Traeth Mawr to the north. At the end of the Cob the train swings north past Boston Lodge works, which takes its name from the lodging house and office built on this site by William Madocks for the workmen engaged in constructing the Cob. It was from here in 1954 that the early preservationists started the gradual process of rebuilding the railway,

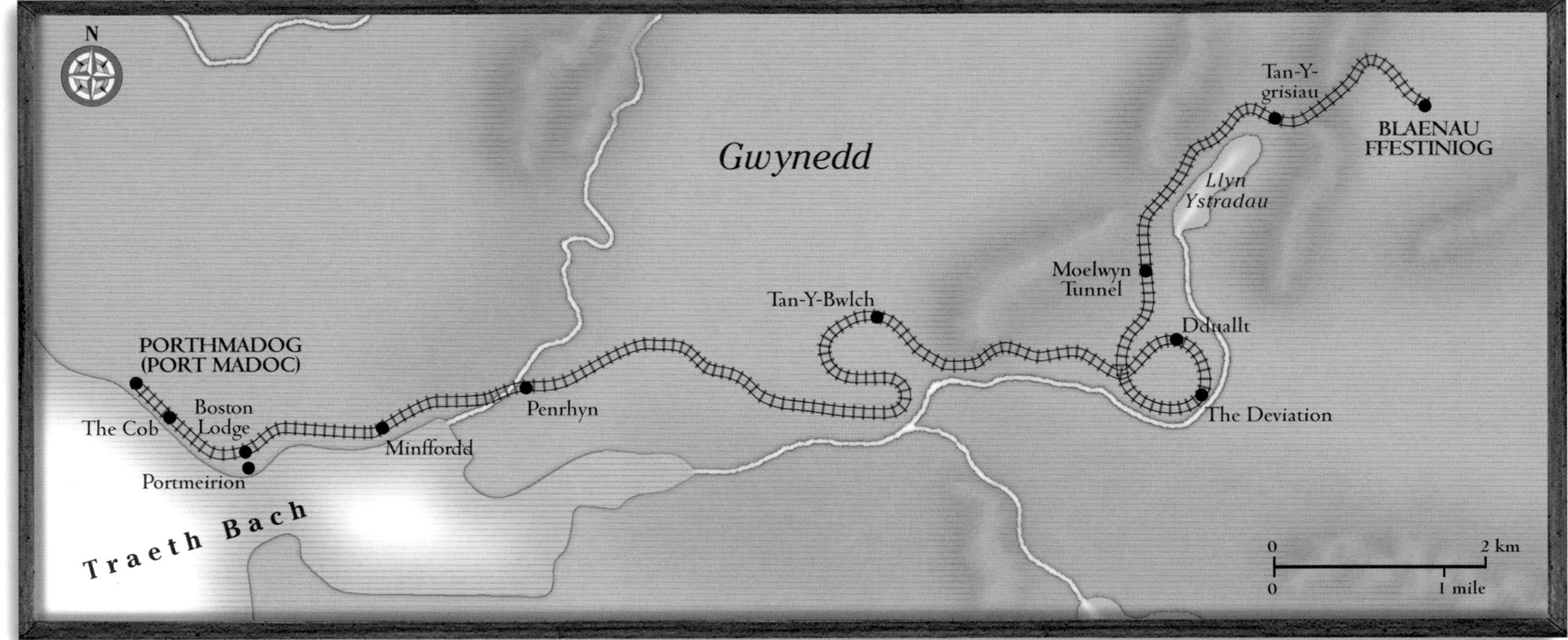

following its closure in 1946 with the decline of the slate industry. From the beginning, Boston Lodge works has been the railway's lifeblood, building some of the locomotives, carriages and wagons and keeping them in good fettle.

A sharpening of the locomotive's exhaust indicates that the climb has already started, to lift the railway from sea level to an elevation of 216m (710ft). The first station at Minffordd became important with the opening in 1867 of the Cambrian Railways' line linking the coast with Shrewsbury. A facility for the transhipment of slate between narrow and standard gauge was developed in the goods yard, and this can still be seen as the train slows for the station and crosses over the Cambrian coast line. Minffordd is also the station closest to William Clough-Ellis's spectacular 'village' of Portmeirion, built from 1926 and now a luxury hotel but also well known as the setting for the 1960s cult television serial, *The Prisoner*.

Once past Penrhyn station and its hostel for FR volunteers, there are few houses, and the views over the rugged, sheep-shorn hills and mountains become progressively more extensive. It is hard to appreciate the scale of some of the stone embankments now that trees have grown up to obscure the views across the loops that the line describes during the climb to the principal intermediate station at Tan-y-Bwlch. The station's refreshment room is popular with walkers, who make use of the train to reach some of the best walking country in Wales.

Leaving Tan-y-Bwlch you can look across the placid waters of Llyn Mair to the line at a lower level on the southern approach to the station. Below is the Oakley Arms Hotel, where the Russian delegation stayed in 1870. Once through the narrow confines of Garnedd Tunnel, there is a spectacular view over the Vale of Ffestiniog as the railway runs along a shelf in the hillside towards Ddault and the start of the 'Deviation'. This was forced on the FR in the mid-1960s when the original trackbed was submerged by the creation of a new reservoir. The challenge of building a new railway, with a spiral to gain height and a 262m (860ft) tunnel, captured the imagination of many who had no particular interest in railways. Consequently the FR was able to build the Deviation using largely volunteer help.

One consequence of the higher-level line is that the final approach to Tanygrisiau station is actually a descent. The slate tips towering above the railway clearly indicate the reason for the line's existence, as it weaves its way through the terraced housing built for the slate workers of Blaenau Ffestiniog. An interchange station with the standard gauge branch line from Llandudno Junction was built near the town centre for the reopening of the last section of the FR, in 1982.

Today another Welsh narrow gauge line is being reopened. This is the Welsh Highland Railway (WHR) from Caernarfon to Porthmadog, where it is intended to restore the connection between the FR and the WHR. One day visitors may be able to enjoy a narrow gauge journey from Caernarfon to Blaenau Ffestiniog, enjoying some of Britain's most impressive mountain scenery from a seat in a restaurant car.

OPPOSITE *Two Fairlie locomotives,* Taliesin *and* David Lloyd George *– the latter a Double Fairlie – line up at Porthmadog for a 1999 heritage gala.*

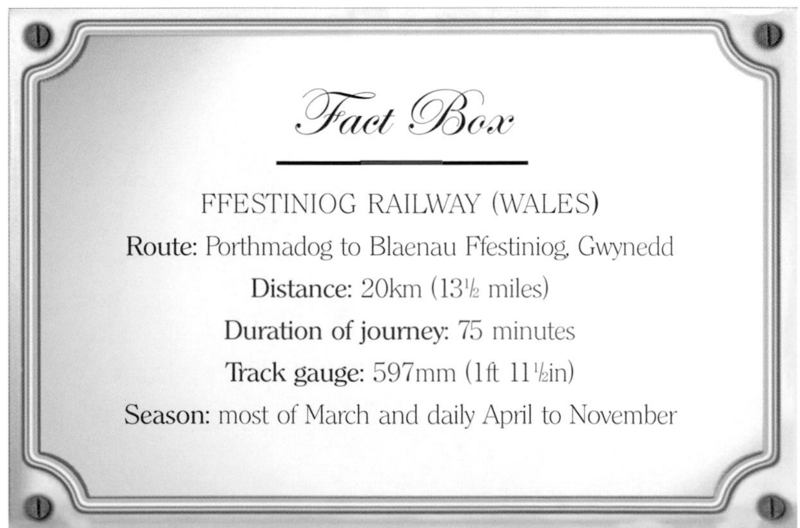

Fact Box

FFESTINIOG RAILWAY (WALES)

Route: Porthmadog to Blaenau Ffestiniog, Gwynedd

Distance: 20km (13½ miles)

Duration of journey: 75 minutes

Track gauge: 597mm (1ft 11½in)

Season: most of March and daily April to November

NORTH YORKSHIRE MOORS RAILWAY

Anthony Lambert

To those who know the North Yorkshire Moors Railway (NYMR), it is no surprise that it carries far more passengers than any other standard gauge heritage railway in Britain, despite its location relatively distant from major conurbations. For the NYMR has the irresistible combination of some of England's most glorious landscapes, a railway full of character – with some fierce gradients that extract stirring sounds from the locomotives – and a long and fascinating history that can also be appreciated on delightful walks.

The 28.8km (18-mile) railway runs from a junction with Network Rail at Grosmont south through Newton Dale to the market town of Pickering. But, periodically, trains run through to the coast at Whitby, and it is with the genesis of the Whitby & Pickering Railway that the story of the NYMR begins. In the early 19th century, Whitby's prosperity as a seaport was reflected in the ability of its wealthier citizens to contribute one-seventh of the capital of the famous Stockton & Darlington Railway (SDR), which opened in 1825. The line's immediate success encouraged Whitby's burghers to think of a railway for their own town, but it took six years of squabbling over the route before it was agreed in 1832 to ask the SDR's engineer, the celebrated George Stephenson (1781–1848), what he thought.

His recommendation of a line to Pickering was adopted, and the railway was rapidly built. It opened in two stages: to Grosmont in 1835 and through to Pickering the following year. Not even London and Birmingham were joined by a railway until 1838, so it was precocious for two such towns to be linked at that

ABOVE *The signal box and level crossing at Levisham, which has featured in a number of film and television productions.*

RIGHT *London & North Eastern V2 2-6-2 No. 60800,* Green Arrow, *at Goathland with a train for Pickering.*

60800
60800

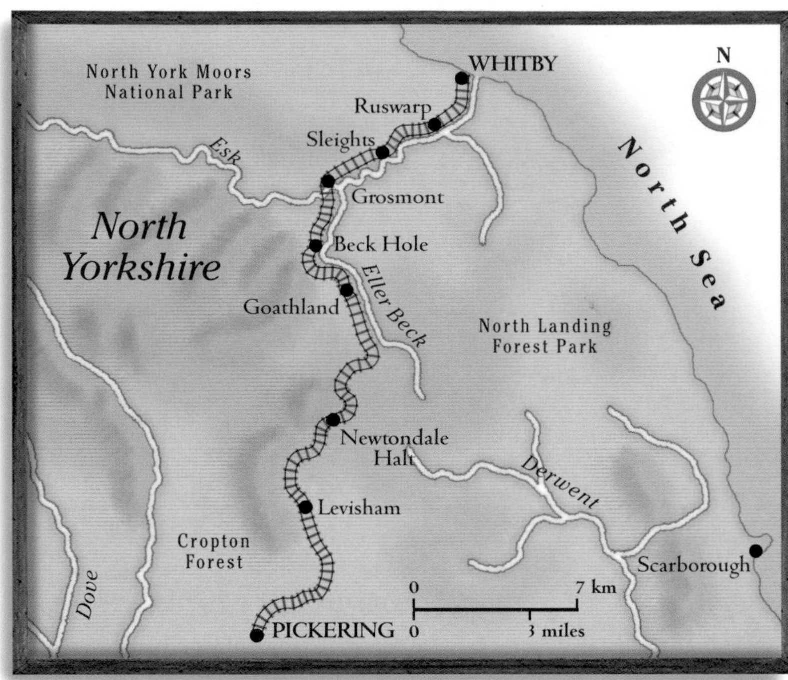

time, even if the initial form of haulage was by horse rather than steam locomotive. The publication in 1836 of a series of engravings, *Scenery of the Whitby & Pickering Railway*, was a measure of the regard in which its landscape was already held.

In addition to horse traction, the Whitby & Pickering Railway (WPR) had a feature that was unusual for any railway in Britain: a rope-worked incline plane for passenger as well as freight traffic. This was forced on the railway by the need to lift the line some 107m (350ft) between Beckholes, at the south end of the tunnel by which the railway escaped from Eskdale, and Goathland. The gradients necessitated by this difference in height would have been too steep for adhesion locomotives of the day even if the WPR had used them elsewhere. Accordingly, Stephenson adopted the water-balanced inclined plane, on which a descending water tank hauled coaches up a 1 in 10 gradient by means of a 15cm (6-inch) hemp rope around a horizontal drum at the summit; the water was emptied at the bottom and the tank had to be returned to the summit by horse. The water system was later superseded by a stationary steam engine.

Horses were replaced by steam locomotives over the sections at each end of the inclined plane in 1847. Various accidents on the inclined plane, including one in which two passengers were killed, encouraged its replacement as soon as locomotives became powerful enough to tackle the 1 in 49 gradient of a new line between Beckholes and Goathland. This was opened in 1865, but seven years later the rails on the incline were relaid to allow testing by the Leeds locomotive builders, Manning Wardle, of some Fell rack locomotives destined for Brazil. Today the incline is a footpath linking the village of Goathland with the hamlet of Beckholes, and the route affords both a pleasant walk and an insight into the history of the railway.

The independent WPR was bought out in 1845 when Pickering was joined to the national network with the opening of a line from York and Malton. In 1854 it became

RIGHT *Two BR 'Standard' 4MT locomotives, 2-6-4T No. 80135 and 2-6-0T No. 76079, pass Darnholm on the climb to Goathland during the Spring Steam Gala held in May 2003.*

80135

part of the mighty North Eastern Railway (NER), and in 1923 of its successor, the London & North Eastern Railway (LNER). Heavy seasonal tourist traffic and a healthy level of freight sustained the line, but its profitability was eventually eroded by road competition. In 1965 both the Pickering/Malton and Scarborough services were withdrawn, leaving Whitby with only one line, the delightful Esk Valley route through Grosmont to Middlesbrough, which remains open. However, there was a strong local feeling that the losses attributed to the Pickering line had been exaggerated to engineer its closure – a common scam of the time to gratify pro-road governments.

Packed public meetings, held to test the level of support for a preservation attempt, led in 1967 to the formation of the North York Moors Railway Preservation Society. It soon became apparent that the cost of buying the railway between Grosmont and Pickering would be beyond the resources of the fledgling society, so attention turned to the Grosmont–Goathland section. Fortuitously, North Yorkshire County Council was more farsighted than the national government and grasped the importance of non-road access to the North Yorkshire Moors National Park, through which almost the entire railway runs. The council agreed to buy the rest of the line and lease it back to the North Yorkshire Moors Railway and, after four years of preparation, it reopened on 22 April 1973.

Though the NYMR begins at Grosmont, some steam-hauled through journeys begin at Whitby, a picturesquely sited town built around the steep cliffs that line both the sea and the River Esk where it meets the North Sea. Victorian and Edwardian Whitby and its environs were immortalized by the outstanding photographs of Frank Sutcliffe (1853–1941), whose work is usually to be found on display somewhere in the town, and also by novelist Bram Stoker (1847–1912), who described Count Dracula landing in England at Whitby in the shape of a wolf, in his novel *Dracula*, published in 1897.

Whitby's Grade II-listed ashlar railway station, built in 1847, stands on the west bank of the river, close to the harbour, and is graced by a five-arched Romanesque portico. It was designed by GT Andrews, whose work for the NER produced some of Britain's most handsome station buildings. Trains for Grosmont leave from here, heading due south before turning with the bends in the river to the west. Beside the line is the disused stone engine shed, also designed by Andrews, which closed in 1959.

Spanning the steep-sided flanks of the narrow Esk Valley and crossing the railway to Grosmont is Larpool Viaduct, a magnificent brick structure of 13 arches built in 1885 to carry the now-closed Scarborough–Whitby–Saltburn line. The line meanders around the hills to the village of Ruswarp, with the Esk still broad and placid enough at this point for rowing boats to be moored along the banks. At Sleights the hills crowd in on the line and the valley narrows, squeezing both railway and river through a gorge. With wheel flanges squealing on the check-railed curves, the train climbs to the junction station of Grosmont, where NYMR trains fork left to enter the valley of the Murk Esk. It is hard to believe that until 1891 there was an ironworks here, on the north side of the railway, that was supplied with locally mined ore; today the site of the blast furnaces is covered by trees.

LEFT *The North Eastern Locomotive Preservation Group's restored North Eastern Railway (NER) 'P3' No. 2392 rests at Pickering after arriving with 'The Moorlander' Pullman dining train, September 2003.*

Leaving the station and passing the recently constructed NER-style signal box, the train enters a double-track tunnel parallel to Stephenson's original tunnel, which had to be abandoned as too small when horses gave way to steam. It is now a footpath to the locomotive works and engine shed which stand at the south end of the tunnel. Here, the NYMR's large fleet of locomotives is maintained and serviced, and where they make use of the overhead mechanical coaling plant which the railway built in 1989 to speed refuelling. The locomotive fleet once worked in all parts of Britain, and contains representatives of all four of the major railway companies that owned the country's railways between 1923 and nationalization in 1948. Among the oldest locomotives is a pair of similar 0-6-2 tank engines built in 1904 and 1909 for Lambton Collieries in the Durham coalfields. These engines delivered wagons laden with coal to the main-line railway, and three of the NYMR's locomotives – heavy NER-designed 0-6-0 and 0-8-0 freight locomotives – were built to take over these workings.

More glamorous are some of the railway's passenger locomotives, such as the LNER A2 Pacific, *Blue Peter*. Having the same name as one of Britain's most successful and long-running children's television programmes gave the locomotive such fame that 60,000 people turned up to see its renaming by the BBC presenters following restoration in 1971. However, like many LNER locomotives, it was actually named after a racehorse. The innovative Pacifics designed for the Southern Railway by Oliver Bulleid (1882–1970) are represented, and the railway even has one of the US Army Transportation Corps' 2-8-0 locomotives, of which over 2100 were built during World War II. The NYMR's example saw service in England, France and Poland before being brought back to England in 1992.

As the driver opens the regulator wide to tackle the bank up to Goathland, the isolated cottages at Beckholes can be seen to the west. The climb through the woods produces a bark from the locomotive, the sound echoing off cutting sides and stone retaining walls. The hills overlooking the line are often crowned by knots of photographers, as the fireman will be shovelling coal for much of the way, producing the ephemeral smoke effects so desired in action pictures. As the train approaches Goathland, so steep is the gradient that only the upper part of the station can be seen.

Generously spread out around sheep-grazed greens, the stone-built village of Goathland is regularly featured in films, such as the Harry Potter adventures, and television series, notably *Heartbeat*. It is a good place to break the journey, both to see the village or enjoy longer walks to the waterfall of Mallyan Spout or one of the best-preserved sections of Roman road in Britain, on Wheeldale Moor. The station, too, has much to offer: a facility for the bottom discharge of coal from a wagon on elevated track has been restored; the goods shed has been cleverly converted into a café with seating areas in open wagons, using sectioned wooden barrels as seats.

Shortly after leaving Goathland the line reaches a summit from which southbound coaches with horses in a 'dandy cart' originally ran by gravity to a point 7.2km (4 miles) north of Pickering, where a horse had to be attached. The transition into the glacier-carved channel of Newton Dale marks a change in the landscape, with deciduous woods giving way to open views across bracken- and heather-covered

RIGHT *The coaling plant at Grosmont engine shed, designed and built by the staff of the NMYR, with visiting London Midland & Southern (LMS) 'Black Five' No. 45407, disguised as No. 45157, beneath it.*

Fact Box

NORTH YORKSHIRE MOORS RAILWAY (ENGLAND)

Route: Grosmont to Pickering, or Whitby, Yorkshire

Distance: 28.8km (18 miles)

Duration of journey: 70 minutes

Track gauge: 1435mm (4ft 8½in)

Season: year round; limited service in winter

moorland. A pair of gatehouses marks the spot at Moorgates where the present route diverges from the original Stephenson line.

Just after the waters of Eller Beck and railway part company, the line describes an S-curve around the 12m (40ft) deep nature reserve of Fen Bogs and Fen Moor, dominated by the precipitous sandstone and limestone escarpments flanking the valley. Visible from here is the monolith that has replaced the 'golf balls' at Fylingdales early warning station, both types of structure an unwelcome intrusion into an area of such natural beauty. The train enters the woods and slows to drop off walkers at Newtondale Halt, accessible only by train and on foot. Emerging from Talbot Wood, the railway skirts Levisham Moor, overlooked by Skelton Tower, built by the Rev. Robert Skelton in about 1850; although it looks like an inspirational place to write a Sunday sermon, it was a place to spend the night after a day's grouse shooting.

Beside the line is The Grange, once the Raindale Inn, where horses replaced gravity as the means of proceeding south to Pickering, while passengers took refreshment. Levisham station is one of the hundreds of stations in Britain that were exasperatingly remote from the village they purported to serve. (The Great Western Railway used to warn of this by adding 'Road' to the name.) Today, the station's remoteness adds to its charm; it lies 90m (300ft) below the village, which is over a mile away; the Station House dates from the building of the original line, in 1836.

Two miles of straight track take the railway past a line of railway cottages at Farwath, followed by the former royal hunting ground of Blansby Park. Twisting through the forest, the railway passes New Bridge signal box (1876), the train slowing for Pickering as it glides beneath the remnants of the Norman castle. Pickering station once had an overall station roof, but it was removed in 1952; today it is a gateway to this historic market town and also houses a tourist information centre. There are hopes that one day the NYMR might be extended south to join up with National Rail at Malton, a development that would add enormously to its transport value and make it by far the longest heritage railway in Britain.

LEFT *The NYMR occasionally operates trains through to Whitby, via the Esk Valley branch. LNER 2-6-4T No. 80135 is shown here leaving Whitby station prior to a journey to Pickering, in April 2003.*

ROMNEY, HYTHE & DYMCHURCH RAILWAY

Anthony Lambert

THERE IS NOTHING LIKE THE ROMNEY, HYTHE & DYMCHURCH RAILWAY anywhere else in the world: only its extraordinary creator has attempted to replicate in miniature – to a gauge of 381mm (15in) – the appearance and atmosphere of a main line railway. And his ability to do that was the result of one of those curious accidents of history that had impossibly unforeseen consequences.

The RHDR's creator was Captain John Edwards Presgrave Howey, born near Woodbridge in Suffolk in 1886. It was Howey's good fortune that, 49 years earlier, his great-uncle Henry had taken the trouble to travel from his New South Wales sheep farm to the embryonic city of Melbourne, Australia, to attend a land auction. There Henry bought a number of plots, most of which he sold on at a good profit, but he still owned three when he and his immediate family were drowned at sea on their way to take up permanent residence in Melbourne.

This land became part of Melbourne's central business district, and it was even said that it was the most valuable area of privately owned urban land in the British Empire. In 1924 it was inherited by JEP Howey, endowing him with sufficient wealth to indulge his passions for speed and things mechanical, which had already found expression in motor racing and steam miniature railways.

ABOVE *The RHDR crest, as carried on the tender of locomotive No. 8* Hurricane, *bears the motto* multum in parvo *(Latin for 'much in little') – appropriate for a miniature railway.*

RIGHT *No. 2* Northern Chief, *a 4-6-2 Pacific built in 1925 and 'sister' of No. 1* Green Goddess, *waits to leave Hythe station with a seasonal special. Both locomotives were commissioned before the completion of the RHDR.*

R.H.D.R.
SANTA SPECIAL
2

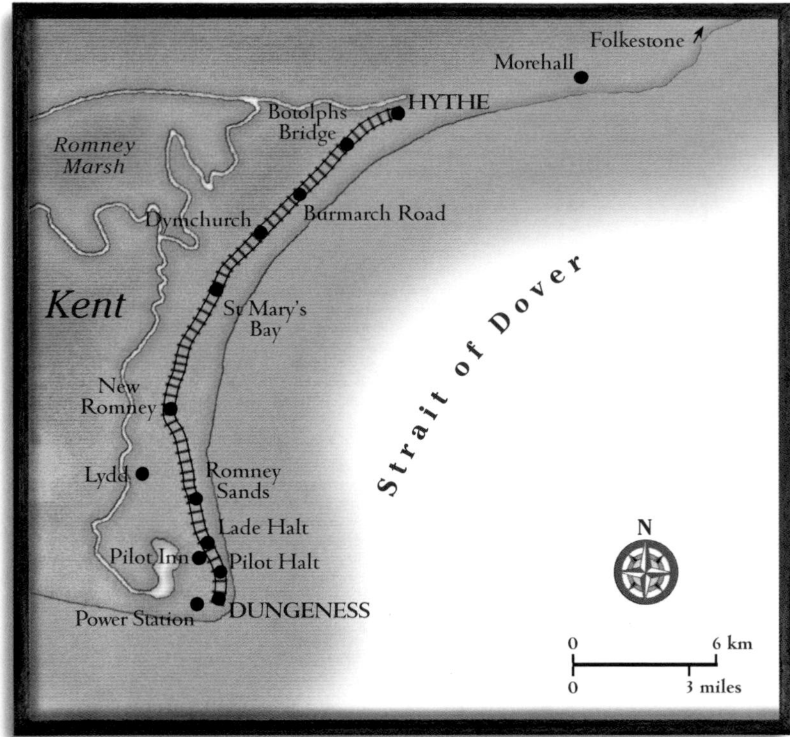

Remarkably the genesis of the idea for a main line in miniature can be traced to a place in London and an event, if not a precise date. A year or two after the end of World War I, two men paid a visit to the Holborn shop of the famous model engineer WJ Bassett-Lowke. One was Grand Duke Dmitri Pavlovitch, a cousin of the deposed Tsar Nicholas II and one of Rasputin's assassins. The other was a scion of the fabulously wealthy Astor family, Count Louis Zborowski, who owned the 23-litre racing car nicknamed 'Chitty-Chitty-Bang-Bang'. The shop assistant later recalled how the two twenty-something men visualized a double-track, properly signalled miniature railway that would allow high-speed running.

The Grand Duke died at Davos, Switzerland, in 1942. But a few years after the Holborn meeting, Zborowski met Howey at Brooklands racing circuit and the two became friends, quickly discovering their mutual interests. Zborowski told Howey of his desire to create a miniature main line, and the two men made a fruitless visit to the Ravenglass & Eskdale Railway in Cumbria with a view to buying it and extending it. They even placed an order for two Henry Greenly-designed 381mm (15in) gauge Pacifics from the Colchester firm of Davey Paxman. But before anything more was done, Zborowski was killed during the 1924 Italian Grand Prix at Monza.

Having recently inherited his father's estate, Howey decided to press on alone, partly with a view to building a railway as a memorial to his late partner. A search for a site that would perform a useful transport function as well as appeal to tourists finally ended in 1925 when Howey went to see the General Manager of the Southern Railway, Sir Herbert Walker. It was Walker who suggested the rough route of today's RHDR – between Hythe and Dungeness – through a part of Kent that is the antithesis of the dramatic Cumbrian fells. This particular corner of the county appears flat to the eye, though there are gentle gradients.

For the impatient Howey this feature was an advantage, since construction over such easy terrain could proceed apace once authority to build the railway had been granted in May 1926. For subsequent managers, the landscape has been less of an asset. No one can pretend that the scenery is a delight to the eye, and the gradual ribbon development of bungalows near the beaches has done nothing to improve it since the railway was built.

But a journey over the railway remains a delightful experience, for Howey succeeded brilliantly in his aim of giving the railway all the character and atmosphere of a scaled-down main line railway. Close your eyes as you bowl along and listen to the throaty exhaust of the locomotive, the deep chime whistle and the rhythmic beat of the rail joints and you can imagine yourself on the main line of the London & North Eastern Railway (LNER) – well, almost. It was the famous Gresley Pacifics of the LNER which Henry Greenly took as the basis for his design, and Sir Nigel Gresley himself visited the railway in 1926 prior to its official opening in July 1927.

Howey ordered five Gresley-inspired Pacifics and two 2-8-2s, so one of them is likely to be at the head of your train. We join the train at the northern terminus of Hythe, a pleasant bus journey along the coast from the port of Folkestone. Hythe was the more genteel of the resorts overlooking the Strait of Dover, its huge Hotel Imperial redolent of evening gowns and hatboxes. With an overall roof spanning the gentle curve of the platforms, the signal-box and signal gantry at the platform end and a small engine shed reached by turntable, Hythe has always been the most attractive of the RHDR's stations.

With a warning whistle from 'the Captain's engine', No. 8 *Hurricane*, to encourage the knot of passengers around the locomotive to take their seats, the train eases out of the station and onto the double track. Immediately beside the railway is the Royal Military Canal, built in 1804–7 as a line of defence against a possible invasion by Napoleon. The train leaves Hythe and heads towards Dymchurch, passing the first of many back gardens to be seen during the journey. Across the open grassland of Romney Marsh to the west is the densely wooded ridge on which stands Lympne Castle, a much-restored, fortified manor house dating from the 14th century that stands out from the trees.

As the pace quickens over the fastest section of the whole railway, the appeal for Howey of this relatively flat countryside is obvious; he would never have been able to achieve such speeds in the Lake District. To indulge his obsession with speed and to haul winter trains, he had a curious-looking machine built using the engine out of his Rolls-Royce Silver Ghost shooting brake. In this contraption he was timed at 96km/h (60¼mph).

The 2-8-2s that Howey ordered were intended to haul ballast traffic from the gravel pits, which are now lakes large enough for sailing, close to the railway on the seaward side. Rattling over girder bridges spanning reed-filled watercourses, the locomotive whistles regularly for level crossings, one of them just before the first station at Dymchurch. Associated with the fictional smuggling parson Dr. Syn, after whom one of the RHDR locomotives is named, the town holds a festival in his memory.

Sheep graze the scrubby fields, which were once covered by guns from the few surviving World War II pillboxes, recalling the RHDR armoured train that was built to patrol the vulnerable coastline. We pass at speed a train hauled by

Winston Churchill, one of the two Canadian Pacific-inspired 4-6-2s; Howey had a CPR footplate pass which he used while crossing Canada on his annual trips out to Melbourne. Entering Jefferstone Lane station, we pass the bungalow that was the home of Edith Nesbit (1858–1924), author of *The Railway Children*.

Rolling into the principal station at New Romney, between the locomotive shed and permanent way yard, we come to a halt beneath the large overall roof. Some people get off to visit the model railway and exhibition about the history of the railway, others entrain for the final section over the single line to Dungeness. Passengers once enjoyed open views of the sea, but the journey now offers an insight into what people do with their back gardens, from creating miniature villages to populating them with gnomes.

With the landing lights of Lydd airport visible to the west, the train finally clears the bungalows and enters the large balloon loop at Dungeness. Tiny wooden huts among the shingle contrast with the immense bulk of the nuclear power station and the slender profiles of the two lighthouses. After a pause at the station, *Hurricane* turns to the north for the return to New Romney and an engine change before the train proceeds back to Hythe.

ABOVE *Locomotive No. 10,* Dr. Syn, *shown waiting to leave Dungeness with a train for Hythe, is one of the RHDR's two Canadian Pacific-style 4-6-2s.*

Fact Box

ROMNEY, HYTHE & DYMCHURCH RAILWAY (ENGLAND)

Route: Hythe to Dungeness, Kent

Distance: 21.6km (13½ miles)

Duration of journey: 65 minutes

Track gauge: 381mm (15in)

Season: daily April to September, and various other weekends

France

CHEMIN DE FER DE LA BAIE DE SOMME

Peter Lemmey

'IL Y A CENT ANS, TOUT ÉTAIT COMME ÇA!' ('A hundred years ago, it was all like this!'), laughed a French holiday-maker as we stood on the swaying front balcony of one of the Baie de Somme line's vintage wooden coaches, enjoying a close-up view of the footplate crew in front of us urging their tank engine along the winding track through the meadows of northern France.

Where the River Somme meets the English Channel, 80km (50 miles) south of Boulogne, it widens into a broad estuary, the Baie de Somme. It is a place of vast skies and distant horizons, with the towns of St. Valery-sur-Somme and Le Crotoy facing each other across the salt marshes and shifting channels of the bay.

St. Valery and Le Crotoy are linked by the metre gauge steam trains of one of France's most attractive preserved railways, the Chemin de Fer de la Baie de Somme. The lines from the two towns meet at a junction called Noyelles inland of the estuary, the interchange with the main SNCF route from Boulogne to Amiens and Paris. On the main line, Boulogne is 45 minutes north of Noyelles, Paris two hours to the south.

The Baie de Somme railway is very much a volunteer operation, and local enthusiasts took over the line immediately after its closure as a public system in 1970. Since then, these weekend workers have restored

ABOVE *The worksplate of locomotive No. 1 bears the name of Corpet Louvet, which produced hundreds of engines for lines all over France.*

RIGHT *The quayside at St. Valery, with a train about to depart for Noyelles. The locomotive was built in Paris in 1906 by Corpet Louvet.*

101

ABOVE *Recalling the heyday of French light railways, engine No. 1 heads through the Picardie countryside between Le Crotoy and Noyelles junction.*

a number of steam engines and rakes of coaches, and their railway has become a hub of tourist activity in the area, carrying 100,000 passengers a year.

While its modern guise is as a cheerful holiday line, the Baie de Somme system is at the same time one of the last survivors of something once common across much of France, the rural light railway, or *secondaire*. In the early 20th century France was covered by a huge network of metre gauge light railways – some 30,000km (18,750 miles) at its greatest extent – with little steam trains all over the country taking local people to market. One or two of the most extensive of the metre gauge systems – the Corsica and Provence lines, for example – still survive, but the authentic local *secondaire* is all but gone. The Baie de Somme line strives hard to create some of the old *secondaire* atmosphere and manages to be a ride into history, as well as great fun.

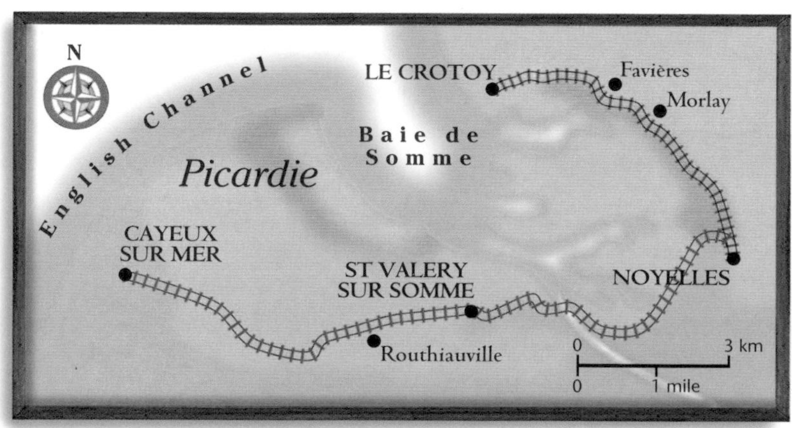

Whether you arrive by SNCF train or along the A16 toll road, Noyelles is likely to be where you first meet the Baie de Somme line. Both rail and road provide glimpses of the bay as you approach, with St. Valery on its hill to the left facing Le Crotoy, with its little harbour, on the right. The metre gauge starts in the yard outside Noyelles SNCF station. The Baie de Somme trains are timed to leave for St. Valery and Le Crotoy simultaneously, the two routes running parallel for a short distance as they leave Noyelles station. The Le Crotoy line – at 6km (3¾ miles) the shorter of the two – heads away round the north side of the bay, in summer sending up clouds of butterflies as it trundles along its narrow gauge course through the pastures.

Rocking and rolling along through rural Picardie, the Le Crotoy train conjures up much of the charm of the old French narrow gauge lines in their prime. During the summer holiday season, trains of six coaches run well filled, with passengers standing out on the coach balconies to enjoy the sun and savour the full smoky sensation of steam haulage. Much of this rolling stock dates back to the 1920s and earlier.

After a last view across the estuary towards distant St. Valery, the train swings across the main road and into Le Crotoy station. The neat station house and goods shed, both sympathetically restored, are typical of those once seen all over light-railway France. Connoisseurs of picturesque railway buildings should not miss Le Crotoy's half-timbered engine shed, where one of the line's locomotives overnights during the busy season. There is time to inspect all these aspects of the station as the engine is turned and watered and then runs round its train to return to Noyelles.

The narrow gauge first reached Le Crotoy and St. Valery in 1887. The railway was promoted by the *département* of the Somme, and formed part of a larger system that served towns and villages inland as well as these two coastal resorts; passengers bound for the seaside have been changing trains at Noyelles for over a century.

The St. Valery line from Noyelles, with its lightly used extension to Cayeux (19km/ 12 miles distant), is the longer of the Baie de Somme's two branches. The line swings away from the Le Crotoy route as it leaves the junction and follows an embankment across the estuary, with the sea visible beyond the salt marshes and sand dunes to

the right. The dyke along which the the train runs was built to replace a long and unreliable timber bridge. From the train, groups of holiday-makers can be seen splashing their way across the bay; one of the attractions of the Baie de Somme is escorted walks across the wide sands from one side of the bay to the other (when the tide is right), with the return leg on the steam train.

Coming off the embankment, the train steams past boatyards and warehouses overlooking the Somme River – which is canalized at this point – followed by the main engine sheds. While the line's original steam engines were pensioned off in the 1950s, the present fleet of chunky, six-coupled tank engines – garnered from expired lines all over northern France (and in one case far beyond) – are very much in the same mould. Regular performers include a 0-6-2T that once worked in the Seine-et-Marne, and three 2-6-0Ts, one of which was exported from France and spent much of its life in America. In 2004, the Baie de Somme line took delivery of an impressive 4-6-0T, a veteran of a metre gauge system in Brittany.

Past the engine sheds the railway bends round onto a narrow bridge over the river's sea-lock; passengers suddenly find themselves looking down onto the yachts moored in St. Valery's marina. A curve to the right brings the line past St. Valery-Ville station and down under the trees by a large ship's chandler to a terminus on the quayside.

Few heritage railways can claim a more picturesque setting than this, with the train framed by period buildings, some half-timbered in the northern French way, and the forest of masts along the quay. In its earlier days the railway was called the *reseau des Bains de Mer* (Sea-Bathers' Railway) on account of the holiday traffic that descended on the line from Picardie, Amiens and even the Paris area, and which the trains shuttled to and from the coastal resorts. The town of St. Valery now sees more visitors even than in those *belle époque* days: as well as the beach at Le Hourdel, the seafood restaurants and the gated old town, it is famed for the shady boardwalk along the estuary, from where William the Conqueror set sail for England in 1066.

The metre gauge doesn't finish at St. Valery; the line heads south from St. Valery-Ville station up over the hill behind the town, past a line of long-abandoned steam engines, and then across country to the quiet coastal resort of Cayeux. Even in high summer the service on this final section is sparse, usually hauled by one of the dumpy 0-6-0 diesel locomotives which were built on the chassis of old steam engines.

Every second year the Baie de Somme holds a steam festival in April; visiting locomotives are brought in from other museum railways, steam-hauled excursions work in to Noyelles on the main line, and the Baie de Somme trains do a roaring trade. Trains have been running round the Somme estuary for well over a century, and are today just as much a part of the holiday scene as they were a hundred years ago. As an excellent example of heritage preservation and 21st-century tourism working in harmony, the Baie de Somme line is hard to beat.

ABOVE *Locomotive No. 15, seen here on the embankment across the Somme estuary, was restored by volunteers after several decades out of use.*

Fact Box

CHEMIN DE FER DE LA BAIE DE SOMME (FRANCE)

Route: Noyelles to St. Valery-sur-Somme and Cayeux, or Le Crotoy, Somme (Picardie region)

Distance: 19km (11¾ miles), or 6km (3¾ miles)

Duration of journey: 3hrs return

Track gauge: 1m (3ft 3⅜in)

Season: Sundays (April to September); daily in July and August (services to Cayeux in summer only)

LE TRAIN DES PIGNES

Peter Lemmey

FRANCE'S CÔTE D'AZUR STRETCHES EASTWARD FROM TOULON TO NICE and the border with Italy. Inland, behind the beaches and boulevards of the Riviera, rise the Alpes Maritimes. Through these craggy mountains flows the River Var, and along the Var valley runs the Chemins de Fer de Provence (Provence Railway), known as the Provence line. The hinterland of the Alpes Maritimes is a hot, hilly landscape of pine-clad uplands and narrow valleys dotted with olive groves. For decades, the metre gauge diesel trains of the Provence line have been a part of the scene. In recent years, however, the billowing coal smoke and shrill whistles of steam traction have made a comeback during the summer months, reviving memories of earlier days.

The Provence line between Nice and the mountain town of Digne provides a spectacular ride, one of France's most scenic rail journeys. The railway's modern diesel railcars reel off the 151km (94 miles) of mountain country in little more than three hours, with numerous viaducts, tunnels and even a spiral along the way. And the reintroduction, since 1980, of steam trains along the railway's middle section – on Sundays from June to mid-October – has added even further to the line's attractions.

The Nice-to-Digne route of today is only a part – albeit a lengthy one – of what was once an extensive metre gauge railway system that spread far across the region. In other parts of France, metre gauge railways were often a branch-line expedient, slow trains for local traffic. But not in Provence. In its early days known

ABOVE *The Provence line's nickname of Le Train des Pignes (Train of the Pine Cones) evokes the pine cone at the centre of its emblem.*

RIGHT *Puget-Théniers station on a summer morning, with the train ready to leave. The wire bonnet on the chimney of E327 is designed to catch sparks and prevent line-side fires.*

CP
E 327

grandly as the Sud-France company, the Provence system was conceived with all the ambition of becoming an important regional network, and by 1911 it had three major routes in operation. Photographs of the time show its elegant 4-6-0 tank locomotives and even some tender engines (very rare for the French metre gauge) on long trains of bogie coaches.

One section of the original Provence system served the Mediterranean littoral between St. Raphaël and Toulon. It was badly mauled during the Allied landings of World War II and finally closed in 1948, its modern diesel railcars finding a new lease of life in Spain. Another leg of the Provence system ran westward from Nice to distant Meyrargues. This line cut across the grain of the country with superb bridges and viaducts, but many of these structures were dynamited in 1944. The trackbed of the Meyrargues line is in some places now a road, in others a cycle way or footpath, still cutting a winding course through the hills.

As well as providing an additional reason for visiting the Nice–Digne line, today's steam trains also convey a flavour of those two lost tentacles of the Provence system in its palmy days. The Digne route of the Provence system managed to survive World War II intact, and is now a go-ahead operation backed by a syndicate of local and regional councils. The full length of the line up through the mountains sees four railcar services each way daily, with a further six trains serving the suburbs of Nice in the lower Var valley. The various tribulations that befell the line in the 1970s prompted the formation of the Groupe d'Étude pour les Chemins de Fer de Provence (GECP) to defend and promote the railway. It was the GECP that was responsible, in 1980, for restoring steam to the line: the Train des Pignes.

Puget-Théniers, 65km (40½ miles) up the Var valley from Nice, is a typical Provençal market town. There was originally a small steam shed here, and in 1977 it became the GECP's choice for its steam base. If in summer you take a Sunday morning stroll through its narrow streets beneath the plane trees, the smell of coal smoke will guide you towards the station and the sight of a volunteer crew preparing their locomotive for the day ahead. The restored engine shed, the nearby turntable and a new carriage shed all bear witness to the efforts of the GECP.

In 1975, when the GECP took the decision to promote a steam train on the Provence line, their major problem was finding some steam power. The Chemins de Fer de Provence had scrapped the last of the 4-6-0 tank engines more than 20 years earlier, and by the 1970s steam power on what remained of the French metre gauge elsewhere had dwindled too. The GECP began a search for a suitable locomotive.

At this point, a lively French narrow gauge enthusiast association, the Federation des Amis des Chemins de Fer Secondaires (FACS) stepped in. They had acquired a metre gauge 4-6-0 tank engine when a group of light lines in Brittany closed in 1969, and were looking for a line on which to exercise it. Built by the Fives-Lille company in 1909, it still carries its original number, E327. This engine has become a mainstay of the Provence steam workings, and indeed it strongly resembles the railway's steam engines of an earlier era.

The GECP has two engines at Puget-Théniers. A regular steam operation like this requires a second locomotive to cover overhaul periods, and in 1986 the group acquired more motive power, this time from Portugal. This was a 2-4-6-0 tank engine, semi-articulated on the Mallet principle, built by Henschel in 1923. After a first career on the sinuous branch lines of the Douro Valley, this impressive engine, with its copper-capped chimney, is now a powerful second string to the GECP's bow.

The usual steam service runs between Puget-Théniers and Annot, a town some 20km (13 miles) further up the valley into the Alps, on three Sundays a month during the summer. Once or twice a year more extensive steam tours are organized over the rest of the Provence line. While some passengers intending to catch the Annot train spend the Saturday night at Puget, the main contingent comes up from Nice for the day on a special connecting working in the form of a diesel locomotive and four modern passenger coaches.

As the steam train is booked to leave Puget-Théniers at 10am, this means an 8am start for passengers from Nice. The metre gauge line climbs steeply through the city suburbs and then, after a tunnel at La Madeleine, drops down into the valley beside the River Var, wide and boulder-strewn at this point. At Lingostière the train skirts the Provence railway's workshops, and at Colomars passes the former junction with the route to Meyrargues, which headed off to the west over the river.

The valley soon closes in and mountain peaks appear ahead. At a number of points along the Var valley, metre gauge feeder routes once came rattling down from the hills to meet the Provence line. Run by a company called the Tramways des Alpes Maritimes, these lightweight branches with their electric cars met the Digne line at Pont Charles Albert, La Vesubie and La Mescla; these services are, of course, long gone and today buses take hikers and holiday-makers up into the highlands.

The connecting diesel train gets in to Puget-Théniers about 20 minutes before the steam train sets off. Although in spring and autumn it can be cooler up here than down on the coast, during high summer it is often quite as hot: there's just time to stroll across the road for a cold drink in the bar. The steam train waits as passengers transfer to its red wooden coaches. Whether headed by E327, the 4-6-0 tank from Brittany, or the Portuguese 2-4-6-0 tank, the train itself pretty accurately re-creates travelling conditions at the beginning of the 20th century.

On the footplate, the volunteer crew are accoutred in the French engineer's traditional blue overalls; their goggles give them a touch of express-train glamour. A final shrill whistle signals the departure, steam jets from the cylinders and the westward journey towards Annot gets under way.

Heading up the valley beside the main road, the locomotive is soon into its stride, the steady steam beat from the chimney audible through the open windows even above the hubbub of a train full of Niçois in high good humour enjoying their day

Fact Box

LE TRAIN DES PIGNES (FRANCE)

Route: Puget-Théniers to Annot, or Digne, Alpes-Maritimes/Alpes-de-Haute-Provence

Distance: 20km (13 miles), 151km (94 miles)

Duration of journey: mid-morning to early evening

Track gauge: 1m (3ft 3⅜in)

Season: most Sundays between June and mid-October

out. On the road alongside car drivers wave and give chase. At this point the train is running along the mid-section of the Provence line. The wooded mountainsides rise to 1500m (4920ft) on either side. Around the 10-km (6-mile) mark, steam is shut off and the train coasts to a halt in Entrevaux station, where we are overtaken in the loop by a Digne-bound railcar. Entrevaux is splendidly fortified – the ancient stone bridge leading directly across to the town's gate is visible from the train. Until 1860 this was the border between the French Republic and the Kingdom of Savoy.

Another shriek from the whistle, a few dawdling passengers scramble on board and the train is away again, straight into a tunnel through a spur of the hillside. From here the gradient steepens to 1 in 45 and the line leaves the road behind as it carves its way along the rocky sides of the valley. It begins to feel like a real mountain railway, the metre gauge curving to and fro up side valleys and across impressive masonry viaducts from which the treetops can be seen below.

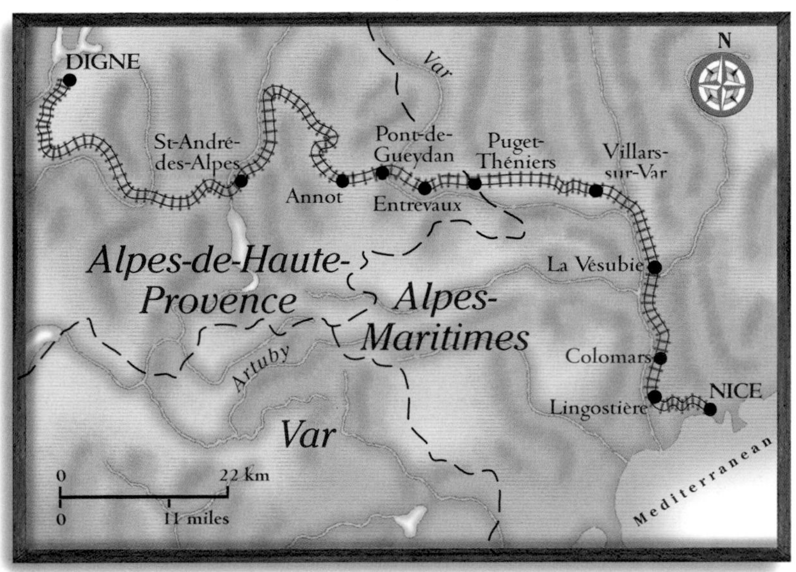

ABOVE *The Train des Pignes takes a breather in Annot, after the strenuous climb up the Var valley from Puget-Théniers.*

All the stations along the valley have the neat buildings so characteristic of French country railways. The train pauses briefly at Pont de Gueydan, where the station looks as though it has hardly changed since the line opened. This was the terminus of another of the ephemeral Tramways des Alpes Maritimes electric lines – this one running up to Guillaumes – which flourished for not much more than a decade.

The sound of the engine is more insistent now as it toils uphill. The train crosses another high viaduct near the halt at Les Scafarels and then, an hour and 40 minutes after leaving Puget-Théniers, the brakes go on for the last time and it rolls into Annot station. This is the limit of regular steam running. West of Annot the Provence line's metals continue through the Alps for another 70km (44 miles) before they finally reach the terminus at Digne. This journey can be done daily by railcar, and – on special runs – the steam train tackles the route too.

Meanwhile the passengers stride into Annot, heading for the cafés and restaurants among the narrow streets and squares of the little mountain town. The engine crew turn and water the locomotive and run it in under the goods shed awning, and then the peace of a hot afternoon descends until 4.30pm and the return run.

Switzerland

DAMPFBAHN FURKA-BERGSTRECKE

Anthony Lambert

Landslides or flooding, causing periodic closures of railway lines, are occupational hazards for railwaymen in many parts of the world. But very few railway lines have to close every winter. Yet the metre gauge (3ft 3⅜in) Furka–Oberalp Bahn (FO) through the Canton of Valais in Switzerland used to have to shut its main line linking Brig with Chur – the route of the world-famous Glacier Express – between October and May because the rack-operated section of line between Oberwald and Realp simply could not be kept open during Alpine winters.

This 18km (11¼-mile) section entailed the scenic climb past the Rhône Glacier, which gave its name to the Glacier Express, to the tunnel under the Furka Pass. Despite its scenic splendour, this line was also one of the most costly sections of railway in the world to maintain. The FO had to devise a bridge that could be removed with the onset of winter snows; otherwise it would not have been fit to carry trains the following spring – if it was there at all – since it lies on an avalanche route; the Steffenbach bridge became famous in its own right, and photographs of the operation to dismantle and re-erect it were often published as an illustration of the power of nature in winter. Moreover, the electrification masts and wires also had to be removed for the winter. Apart from being a major impediment to travel, the closure meant a severe loss of

ABOVE *A jauntily attired train crew shovel coal into the firebox. Passengers can stand on the balcony of the end coach and watch the crew at work.*

RIGHT *At the railway's maintenance base in Realp, workers swing round locomotive No. 6* Weisshorn*, built in 1902 by SLM.*

6
WEISSHORN
85

ABOVE *A sightseeing train approaches the terminus at Gletsch. In the background is the switchback road that climbs to the Grimselpass.*

OPPOSITE *Festooned with garlands of flowers, locomotive No. 1* Furkahorn *emerges from a tunnel.*

revenue. It was to allow year-round operations over this vital artery that the FO built a 15.4km (9½-mile) base tunnel between Oberwald and Realp. The tunnel was opened in June 1982, and the last train over the old route ran in October 1981.

This would have been the end of the story of a remarkable if burdensome section of railway had it not been for the efforts of an enthusiasts' association which was formed in 1983 with a view to the progressive reopening of the line from the Realp end using steam traction (the main line had been electrified in 1940–2). Three years later a company, the Dampfbahn Furka-Bergstrecke (Furka Cogwheel Railway) – DFB for short – was incorporated by the association to carry out its intentions. However, much work on the track and structures was required.

From the start the DFB knew that it would have to find a source of steam locomotives if its plans were to be fulfilled. Thoughts turned to the astonishing history of the 10 rack locomotives built in 1913–14 by the Swiss Locomotive & Machine (SLM) works in Winterthur for the Brig–Furka–Disentis Bahn (BFD), predecessor of the FO. These had been made redundant by the electrification of the FO in 1942; four had been retained for snowplough duties and work on dismantling the electrification catenary before winter, and four were sold in 1947 to the Indo China Railway in what is now Vietnam. They were to be used between Thap-Chàm and Da-Làt, on which there were some rack sections with grades comparable to the FO. The railway suffered during the Vietnam War and after closure quickly became overgrown.

Correspondence with the Swiss embassy in Hanoi failed to establish whether the locomotives had survived, but then a railway enthusiast returned from Vietnam with photographs of them in their jungle setting. Thanks to the good offices of the Swiss ambassador, a team from the DFB visited Vietnam in 1988 and found not only the four rack locomotives but also four larger 0-8-0 tanks, survivors of three batches of nine locomotives built by SLM and Esslingen Engineering. Two years of negotiations followed, and a deal was done for all four rack locomotives, two of the 0-8-0s and various wagons and spare parts. The cost was SFr 1.4 million plus a further SFr 500,000 for transport.

The story of how a 12-man team from the DFB went out to Vietnam in 1990 to organize their retrieval from the jungle is an epic. For instance, one bridge on the road to the main-line railhead was so weak that it could not take the weight. Consequently each locomotive had to be unloaded from the road trailer in the middle of the jungle, often in torrential rain, and pushed across an adjacent railway bridge and reloaded on

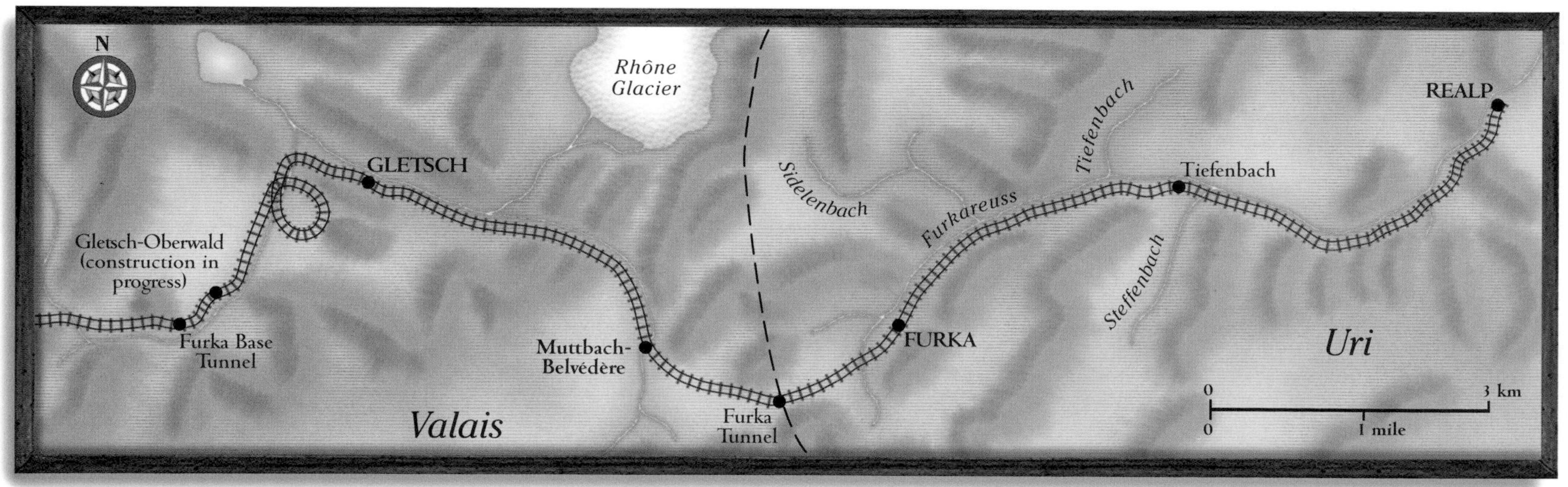

to the trailer. Eventually the cargo was loaded on to a ship for Hamburg and the return to Switzerland. Two were shipped via the former East German State Railway works at Meiningen in Thuringia, which restored them to working order.

Meanwhile in 1988 the town of Chur had donated the DFB's first steam locomotive, the former Brig–Visp–Zermatt Bahn (BVZ) No. 6 *Weisshorn* of 1902, for which a new three-road engine shed at Realp was opened in 1990. The first part of the line was reopened to passengers as far as Tiefenbach in 1992, with the next section to Furka station, on the east side of the tunnel, the following year. The major advance came in July 2000 with the reopening of the Furka Tunnel and the dramatic stretch past the Rhône Glacier to Gletsch. The date chosen was 14 July – Bastille Day – because the line had originally been built by a French company.

Three serviceable steam locomotives make up the DFB's current fleet: the two former Vietnam/FO 2-6-0 tanks, No. 1 *Furkahorn*, built by SLM in 1913 and No. 2 *Gletschhorn* (SLM 1914); and 0-4-2T No. 6 *Weisshorn*, built by SLM in 1902 for the BVZ. The two 0-8-0 tanks from Vietnam await restoration to working order. The railway has a collection of historic coaches, the oldest dating from 1903. They include a buffet car, which was rebuilt by volunteers from a 1916 built service vehicle used on the Solothum–Zollikofen–Bern Bahn. Besides the conventional carriages, it has four open, panoramic coaches for use when the weather is fine.

The best way to reach the DFB is via the wonderfully scenic railway between Brig and Chur, on which there is never a dull moment. The DFB station at Realp is a short walk from the Matterhorn Gotthard Bahn (the new name of the FO and BVZ, which merged in January 2003) and has two platforms and a bay.

There is no rack to begin with, but it is not long before the distinctive clunk of the cog wheel engaging the rack is heard and the gradient steepens to 1 in 9. The exhaust beat from the locomotive changes as it switches over to compound working, whereby the steam is used twice, first in the high-pressure rack cylinders and then in the low-pressure outside cylinders driving the wheels.

The scenery is reminiscent of a Scottish Highland glen, with the steep-sided hills covered by coarse grasses and rock outcrops and dissected by streams flowing into the Furkareuss River. On cold damp days, the white smoke from the locomotive hangs in the air, coalescing with the mist or low cloud. Hardly a building is to be seen all the way up the valley. Before reaching the first station at Tiefenbach, the train passes through several short tunnels and crosses the Steffenbach bridge. There is a pause at the station to allow the crew to replenish the locomotive's water tanks which are quickly depleted by the rack sections.

At Furka there is a wait while passengers buy a warming beverage at the café. At 2160m (7087ft) above sea level, Furka station is an austere place, the station building and buffet being set into the hillside to provide some protection from the cold, winds and snow. The train then negotiates the 1874m (6148ft) Furka tunnel under the pass, emerging at the appropriately named Muttbach-Belvédère station and beginning the descent to Gletsch, the present terminus. To the north the Rhône Glacier can be seen, though its extensive retreat, documented since the first Glacier Express ran in 1930, is a shocking reminder of the impact of global warming.

Ahead the switchback road that climbs from Oberwald and Gletsch to Meiringen can be seen climbing to the Grimselpass, while the few buildings that form the village of Gletsch seem like tiny models beneath the ring of mountains. Gletsch was the terminus of the line from Brig between 1913 and 1925, which must have been wonderful for business at Gletsch's only hotel, the Glacier du Rhône. It is worth wandering along to have lunch at the hotel, one of Switzerland's most unspoilt. Its huge dining room and marvellous period atmosphere are redolent of the days of label-encrusted leather cases, Homburg hats and Thomas Cook itineraries.

Fact Box

DAMPFBAHN FURKA-BERGSTRECKE (SWITZERLAND)

Route: Realp to Gletsch, Valais/Uri cantons

Distance: 12.6km (8 miles)

Duration of journey: 110 minutes

Track gauge: 1m (3ft 3⅜in)

Season: late June to early October

Germany

BAD DOBERAN–KÜHLUNGSBORN WEST

Anthony Lambert

FEW RAILWAYS CAN BE SAID TO OWE THEIR ORIGINS TO THE ADVICE of a physician, but that is the case for the narrow gauge branch line that runs along Germany's Baltic coast between the spa town of Bad Doberan and the resort of Kühlungsborn West. Professor Dr. Samuel Vogel advised Duke Friedrich Franz I of Mecklenburg-Schwerin to take up sea bathing for the sake of his health, and the place chosen by the duke was Heiligendamm. Founded in 1793, it became known as 'the white town by the sea' and is the oldest spa of its kind in Germany.

With the railway age, it was inevitable that the spa's fashionable clientele should expect to reach its doors by a form of transport faster and more comfortable than a horse-drawn carriage. Accordingly, in 1886 a line built to the rare gauge of 900mm (2ft 11½in) was opened from a junction with the standard gauge railway between Rostock and Wismar at Bad Doberan to Heiligendamm, with the terminus being a minute's walk from the spa. It took just seven weeks to build the 6.6km (4-mile) line, thanks to the easy, largely flat terrain which required no bridges, tunnels or engineering works beyond simple grading of the trackbed. At first, tram engines were used, with 'skirts' over the wheels and motion to minimize the risk of a passing crinoline being caught up in revolving steel.

ABOVE *The platform at Bad Doberan station, where passengers make the easy cross-platform change from standard gauge to narrow gauge.*

RIGHT *One of the railway's three 2-8-2Ts of 1932, No. 99.2321-0, threads its way through the streets of Bad Doberan on its way to the Baltic.*

BAD DOBERAN-KÜHLUNGSBORN WEST, GERMANY

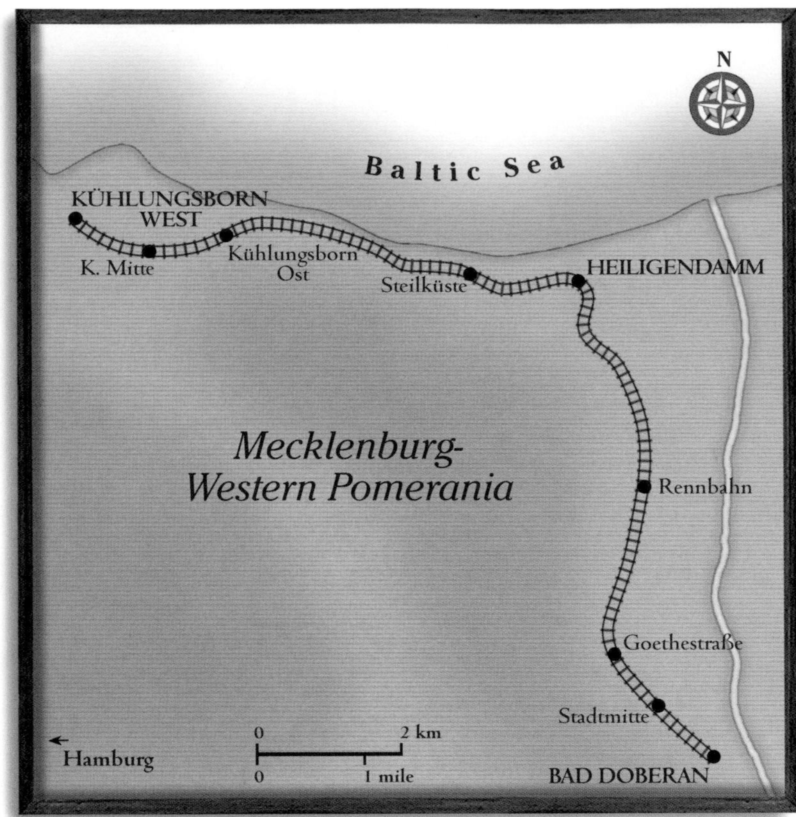

Twenty-four years later, the line was extended to Brunshaupten (today's Kühlungsborn Ost) and Arendsee (Kühlungsborn West), deviating from the existing route just before the terminus at Heiligendamm and so requiring a replacement station there. The line became part of German Railways in 1920, but plans to convert the line to standard gauge were dropped during the Depression. Its location near a tourist area, coupled with its usefulness to local communities, enabled the line to survive closure attempts during the post-World War II era when Germany was divided and the line lay in the GDR. Today the railway is called the Mecklenburgische Bäderbahn Molli GmbH. & Co. (MBM), but is referred to simply as the 'Molli'.

The Molli's most delightful feature nearly proved its undoing. Trains trundling along the street, whistles blowing or bells ringing, were once a common sight in the United States, South America, Indonesia and South Africa, but – trams apart – it was never common practice in Europe. Today it is extremely rare, and the Molli is one of the very last railways to share road space with pedestrians and road traffic. The East German administration recognized the value of the railway in 1976, when they declared it a national monument, but some dull souls tried to do away with the street-running sections during the last years of the Iron Curtain. However, the Molli survived until reunification and wiser counsels have since prevailed.

The railway is recognized as a great asset to the area, not only as an attraction in its own right but also because it helps visitors and local people travel about – on the train, shopping baskets are almost as common as rucksacks and cameras. The popularity of the area with holiday-makers helps to fill the long trains, and special excursions using historic carriages or a bar car can often be seen, perhaps hauled by the least powerful locomotive on the railway, a 0-8-0 tank built by VEB Locomotivbau Karl Marx, Babelsberg, in 1951. Most trains are in the hands of a trio of large 2-8-2 tanks built in 1932 by Orenstein & Koppel in Berlin. All locomotives face Bad Doberan, and the open-balconied red-and-cream coaches allow passengers to stand close to the chimney on westbound trains and enjoy the sound of the locomotive's exhaust.

From the junction station, with its cross-platform change, trains for Kühlungsborn West skirt a well-wooded park, curving down towards the town centre and crossing the main square to dive down Goethestrasse, a shopping street now shared only with pedestrians. Gingerly passing café tables and racks of clothes and newspapers, the train pauses at Stadtmitte station close to the theatre and tourist information office. On the eastbound journey, the guard operates the traffic lights here to allow the train to cross the road junction at the square.

It is well worth exploring Bad Doberan on foot to appreciate its wealth of historic buildings, notably the 14th-century Münster (cathedral), described as one of the most beautiful Gothic brick buildings in northern Germany. The Münster cannot be seen from the train, but its secular equivalent can – a 19th-century Gothic school in red brick with a cathedral-like rose window and decorative machicolations up the gables.

Fact Box

BAD DOBERAN–KÜHLUNGSBORN WEST (GERMANY)

Route: Bad Doberan to Kühlungsborn West, Mecklenburg-Western Pomerania

Distance: 15.4km (9½ miles)

Duration of journey: 40 minutes

Track gauge: 900mm (2ft 11½in)

Season: year round

LEFT *An early afternoon working from Kühlungsborn West, hauled by the Molli's 2-8-2T No. 99.2321-0, enters the station at Bad Doberan.*

Leaving the central streets, the railway passes rows of elegant villas, some neo-classical in style, others Gothic with Italianate towers and ornate brickwork, and a few with Art Deco touches. Once out of the town, the railway parallels the road and enjoys the shade of the magnificent avenues of lime trees that line the road for much of the way to the perimeter of the woodland surrounding Heiligendamm. A racecourse and fields border the railway, and trains make special stops here during race meetings.

The train enters the station and passing loop at Heiligendamm, where the pedimented, white-stucco station of 1934–5 has been restored. As the train negotiates the level crossing to the west of the station, passengers can glimpse the various buildings of the spa. Although built between 1796 and 1910, the principal buildings are a remarkably homogeneous group, blending well with the smaller villas that are along the coast to the east. Over the years, Heiligendamm became very fashionable, attracting such figures as Tsar Nicholas I, Field Marshal Blücher (of Waterloo fame), Mendelssohn, Proust and Queen Louise of Prussia. During the communist era, the hotel and spa were used as a sanatorium, and since reunification the main buildings have been restored and reopened in 2003 as a five-star Kempinski hotel. To the west beyond the pier lies wooded coastline extending as far as the eye can see.

The line climbs away from Heiligendamm, calling for noisy exertion from the locomotive. In the trees beside the line is a tiny chapel that was once part of the spa. As the railway leaves the beech woods, the views to the south open out to vast, rolling fields broken up by tree-fringed roads and the occasional clump of trees, often screening a hunter's elevated hide. A target, in the form of deer, can sometimes be seen grazing, oblivious to the train's passage or their peril. A small harbour gives a hint of the sea but the railway stays away from the shoreline, preferring a route through the apple trees that seem to fill every back garden in Kühlungsborn and again trundling through some streets of the resort, which is famous for its Art Deco buildings.

The size of Kühlungsborn Ost station is indicative of the crowds that flock to the beaches in summer, and the passage through the town exemplifies the care and pride so characteristic of many German municipalities: abundant trees, off-road cycle routes, even a duck pond with refuges for the birds. A brief interlude of fields separates Kühlungsborn Ost from Kühlungsborn Mitte station, with its neat shelter and nearby thatched house. The plain brick station building at Kühlungsborn West, relieved by indented courses of brickwork, contains a café and adjacent museum displaying lamps, whistles, worksplates, old photographs and a video about the Molli. Outside, trackwork, signalling equipment and a sectioned boiler are arranged in a small park beside the inoperable 0-8-0T No. 99.2332, sister engine to No. 99.2331. The pair was built to operate the railway at a uranium mine in Saxony; when the mine closed, the rarity of 900mm gauge locomotives gave them a second lease of life on the Molli.

The locomotive shed (built in 1922) and carriage shed (built in 1915) stand opposite the station, the latter protecting the vintage coaches and the surplus stock from the elements, particularly in winter (when trains are less than half the length of summer workings). From here it is only a short stroll to the beach, its tree-lined promenade and the large villas that the Molli was extended to serve.

RÜGENSCHE KLEINBAHN

ANTHONY LAMBERT

The island of Rügen, 962sq km (2492 sq miles) in area, lies off the Baltic coast, and is linked to the mainland by a bridge and causeway from Stralsund. For centuries, Rügen's natural beauty and picturesque coastline have drawn visitors – from Bismarck and Brahms to Einstein and Thomas Mann. Tourism has long been the mainstay of the local economy, and at one time the island had an extensive network of 750mm (2ft 5½in) gauge lines connecting with the standard gauge railway network. The latter survives intact, but all that is left of the former is the 24.2km (15-mile) section of the Rügensche Kleinbahn (RüKB) between Göhren and Putbus with a further seasonal 2.6km (1½-mile) extension to Lauterbach Mole.

The line opened in stages between 1895 and 1899 and is much more heavily engineered than the neighbouring Molli (*see* pp84–7), with deep cuttings and heavy embankments. During the communist era, the railway continued to carry a heavy passenger traffic, although there were rumours of closure in the mid-1970s. Now popularly known as Der Rasender Roland, or 'Raging Roland', the railway has taken on a new lease of life since German reunification, with impressive investment made in all aspects of its operation.

The RüKB still has two original Rügen locomotives, a pair of 0-8-0 tank locomotives built by Vulcan of Stettin in 1914 and 1925. The remainder of the locomotive fleet has been gathered from other narrow gauge lines and includes three big 2-10-2 tanks built in 1953 by VEB Locomotivbau Karl Marx, Babelsberg, and a pair of 2-8-0 tanks built in 1938 by Henschel for the Kleinbahn Kreis Jerichow I

ABOVE *The open balconies and sliding end doors allow passengers in the leading coach to enjoy the sight and full sound of the locomotive.*

RIGHT *Locomotive No. 99.783, one of the line's two 1950s-vintage East German 2-10-2 tanks, rounds a curve near the halt at Jagdschloss.*

99 783
50
99 783

near Magdeburg in Saxony. There is also a changing collection of privately owned locomotives that sees occasional use. All locomotives face Putbus.

In winter the green and cream carriages are supplied with buckets of brown coal briquettes to feed the solid-fuel stoves for heating, creating the curious sight of sparks emanating from carriage chimneys as coal is thrown on the fire. The carriages have end balconies, so passengers can enjoy the open air as well as the sound of the locomotive. In high season some trains have a buffet car and most have up to two vans for carrying bicycles; Rügen's gentle gradients and network of dedicated bike routes makes cycling a popular way of exploring the island. There is also a set of historic coaches, in the RüKB's traditional brown livery, used for charter trains.

Most passengers begin their journey midway along the line in Binz, the island's largest and most celebrated resort. Built in the late 19th century in a style known as Bäderarchitektur (spa architecture), the pine-sheltered villas with frilly woodwork and decorative wrought-iron balconies and loggias overlook the gentle curve of a bay. The land rises to wooded cliffs to the east. Situated on the outskirts of the town, the RüKB station building overlooks three platforms and was completely remodelled in 2003–4.

Eastbound trains for Göhren face a stiff climb past trim allotments with chalet-style summer-houses and through bracken and birch-lined cuttings into the beech woods of Granitz Forest. Deep in the woods is the first halt, at Jagdschloss, situated on a sharp S-bend. It is used by the many people making the pleasant walk through the woods to the summit of the Tempelberg, upon which stands Jagdschloss Granitz, a colossal brick hunting lodge built by Prince Wilhelm Malte of Putbus. This square Gothic Revival building with four cylindrical corner towers was begun in 1837 and finished nine years later. It is dominated by a central round tower with a belvedere reached by a vertigo-inducing, wrought-iron staircase of 154 steps cantilevered out from the circular walls. On a clear day visitors are rewarded with spectacular views over eastern Rügen from the 38m-high (125ft) platform.

Leaving Jagdschloss the train soon reaches the summit in a deep cutting, from which it descends through birch woods to the isolated passing loop and station at Garftitz, reached on foot by a timeless unpaved track through an avenue of trees. Gently undulating farmland drops down to the sea and one of the deep inlets that characterize the coastline of Rügen, the Sellinersee, providing a harbour for yachts.

After pausing at the new woodland halt of Sellin West, the train descends through open country past a vast holiday development to Sellin Ost, where waiting passengers can patronize the café in the new station building. After the halt at Baabe, the railway again enters woodland, with oak and birch trees flanking the line all the way to Göhren. The terminus is so hemmed in by forest that there is not a hint of the maritime location, even though it is only a short walk from the sea and serves a pleasant resort with no less than four museums: a 19th-century farmhouse, a local history collection, a farm museum and a boat that carried freight around Rügen.

Fact Box

RÜGENSCHE KLEINBAHN (GERMANY)

Route: Göhren to Putbus, or Lauterbach Mole, Rügen Island, Mecklenburg-Western Pomerania

Distance: 24km (15 miles)

Duration of journey: 84 minutes

Track gauge: 750mm (2ft 5½in)

Season: year round; limited service in winter

ABOVE *Although traffic is heaviest during the busy summer season, the Rügensche Kleinbahn runs limited services in winter.*

OPPOSITE *The picturesque main square of Putbus, laid out during the 19th century as the focus of the royal capital of the Prince of Putbus.*

Returning westward to Binz, the tower of Jagdschloss stands out above the surrounding trees in its commanding position atop the 107m (351ft) hill. Turning southwest from Binz, the line weaves a course through rolling hills of mixed farming, including a geese farm. Again there is an almost timeless air to some of the rural buildings, which often feature thatched roofs. A few even betray in their details the period when Sweden controlled Rügen, between 1648 and 1815. Deer forage in the fields and are accustomed to the frequent passage of the train.

The pretty rural setting of the station at Posewald has been enhanced by tree planting, and a board describes local walks. Fields of brassicas precede the arrival at Putbus, and to the west a tall embankment can be seen; this once carried the long narrow gauge line that went through the island's oldest town, Garz, to a junction with the standard gauge at Altefähr, close by the bridge to the mainland. Local government proposals in the early 1990s to reopen this and the Bergen–Altenkirchen line sadly came to naught. Before the train draws alongside the standard gauge branch line from Bergen, the land between the lines is occupied by a private railway museum, the Pommersches Kleinbahnmuseum (Pomeranian Narrow Gauge Museum), with 0-6-0 tender tank No. 99.4652 *Frank S*, built by Henschel in 1941, and a fine collection of rolling stock. There is also a section of 600mm (1ft 11⅝in) gauge track with stub point and wagons to illustrate the basic industrial railway. At the south end of the extensive station is the narrow gauge engine shed and workshop, and the exit to the town is through the standard gauge building with its attractive wooden canopy.

Putbus is a remarkable place, the last European town to be planned as a royal seat. It was created by the builder of Jagdschloss Granitz, Prince Wilhelm Malte of Putbus. Most of the elegant neoclassical buildings around the market square and the Circus, with its radiating gravel paths and avenues of trees, are painted white and gleam in the sunshine. Just off the square is Rügen's only theatre, built in 1819–21 as a place of entertainment for the Prince's guests. The portico overlooks a 70ha (173-acre) park begun in 1725 and altered into an English-style landscape garden in the early 19th century. All residents of the town were welcome to enjoy it.

Narrow gauge trains were extended on 30 May 1999 along the standard gauge line from Putbus to Lauterbach Mole, thanks to the insertion of a third rail to create mixed gauge track. RüKB trains run beyond Putbus only between June and mid-September, obviating the need for passengers to change trains to reach the sea. However, these trains have to be push/pull operated since there is no run-round loop at Lauterbach Mole; some trains have a diesel and steam locomotive at each end. A new station has been built adjacent to the harbour, which offers boat connections to the tiny island of Vilm, which is a biosphere reserve.

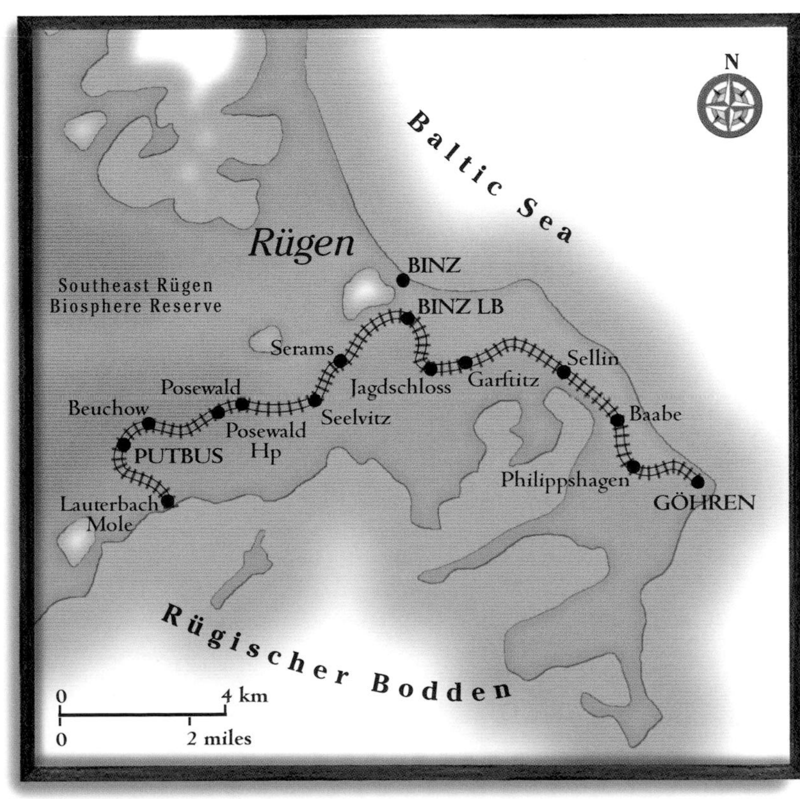

Poland

WOLSZTYN TO POZNAN

Ailsa Camm

IN THE DARKNESS BEFORE DAWN, a streetlamp picks out the glistening cobbles of a rain-washed street. It is 3.45am in the morning. The houses are silent, blinds resolutely drawn. One or two yellow squares punctuate the gloom – early risers preparing for the journey to work. Outside, small groups of people make their way to the station, trailing muffled conversation and cigarette smoke.

As they approach the level crossing, the silence is broken by the 'pop' of a whistle. A smell of coal dust pervades the air. Waiting patiently at the end of the platform is the 4.16am to Poznan, its bulk half-obscured by the blackness, its headlamps silvering needles of rain. There is a sense of imminent departure, of mounting excitement in the thump-thump of the air-brake compressor and the rising tide of steam shrouding the platform canopy's iron curlicues.

This is Wolsztyn, a small Polish town on the plain that links Wielkopolska province to the German border. The scene may recall wartime Central Europe, but it is resolutely 21st century. If the departure of a steam train can ever be described as mundane, in this corner of Poland it is precisely that. The passengers are real people going to real jobs; the engines pulling their carriages are functional machines. They are all that remain of the army of steam locomotives built after World War II to revive Poland's shattered economy.

ABOVE *Veteran Polish crews provide training for the growing numbers of foreigners who come to Wolsztyn to experience driving a steam locomotive.*

RIGHT *On a cold winter morning a Poznan-bound passenger train traverses the frozen terrain of Wielkopolska province.*

WOLSZTYN TO POZNAN, POLAND

These, the last scheduled steam trains in Europe, owe their survival to a mixture of luck and tenacity. During the Soviet era, when the town was an important military transport base, coal-fired traction was kept on, as insurance against threatened oil supplies, long after it had disappeared from other parts of Poland.

Even in Wolsztyn, steam traction would now be a distant memory but for the determination of an expatriate British steam fanatic. Since 1997, Howard Jones has kept the Wolsztyn shed alive through an arrangement with its owner-operators, the Polish State Railways. He subsidizes the extra costs of running the fleet of steam locomotives with money that enthusiasts from all parts of the globe pay to drive steam trains under the supervision of their professional crews.

Wolsztyn is at the hub of five lines radiating out through the forests and meadows of what was once part of greater Prussia. Six steam-hauled passenger services leave the station each day. Some clatter northeast to the modern city of Poznan; others make for the gabled market town of Lezno further south and a few head northwest to industrial Zbaszynek, through which the Berlin–Warsaw express tears at alarming speed. The other two lines trundle through the wooded heathlands to Nowa Sól and Sulechow, and are exclusively freight-operated.

There is a reassuring clunk as the signal arm lifts skyward and the Poznan train, with its olive-grey double-decker carriages, moves off, sliding past the Prussian-built signal boxes standing sentinel at either end of the station. A hundred years old, their German-built lever frames are still fully operational. Opposite is the busy locomotive depot, perhaps the most eloquent proof that this is a living, breathing line. As the train gathers speed, there is just time to take in the semicircular shed with its stud of black Ol49s raising steam in the shadows, the legions of overalled mechanics, the conveyor belt disgorging lumps of coal into a small wagon, the drivers and firemen saluting each other as they come off shift or report for duty – the first grimy with soot, the second laden with soup and sausages for the outward journey.

The depot at Wolsztyn, which has been working under the same regime for nearly a century, houses around 30 locomotives of 13 different classes. They range from the oldest, the Tki3-87 dating back to 1908, to the most glamorous, the green and black Pm36-2, *Piekna Helena* (Beautiful Helen), which burns a staggering 17 tons of coal on its 313km (185-mile) 'seaside' excursions to the port of Gdansk.

The 80km (50-mile) journey from Wolsztyn to Poznan crosses the great Prussian plain, a kaleidoscope of brooding forests, verdant meadows and vast, tussocky heaths. Though only 225km (140 miles) from Berlin and 370km (230 miles) from Warsaw, this is deeply rural country, where ploughshares dot the fields and the rasp of the corncrake can be heard on a summer evening. Hundreds of country roads intersect the railway line, which was built in the 1890s as a means of transport for the farming population and as a way of moving agricultural produce to market.

There are 15 stations on the single track between Wolsztyn and Poznan, and on the clear stretches in between, the engine is pushed hard to to make up for the many speed restrictions that beset the line. The workhorses of the Wolsztyn network, the Ol49 2-6-2 class, are perfect for the job. With a rugged simplicity rendered almost

RIGHT *Early morning at Wolsztyn depot, with workers preparing a steam locomotive for another day. The cost of operating steam in Poland is offset by the income brought in by rail enthusiasts and tourists.*

brutish by their trademark hooded smoke deflectors, these 1950s-vintage locomotives are a favourite with their crews, being easy to maintain and endlessly forgiving.

Foresters' huts and weather-boarded windmills flash by as Ol49-59 reaches 110kph (70 mph), whistling furiously as it gallops towards one gateless crossing after another. For much of the time it runs neck and neck with trucks bound for Poznan and death-defying Trabants intent on beating it to the next level crossing. In the early morning light, with smoke piling out behind, the shadow of the locomotive dances across a landscape dappled with lakes and villages bearing romantic, unpronounceable names: Rostarzewo, Drzymalowo, Ruchocice. On the far horizon, the twin spires of a Baroque seminary tower over the cornfields; in the middle distance, the overgrown garden of a once thriving estate, abandoned in the chaos following World War II.

The first stop, Tloki, is typical of many of the remote country stations along the line. Silent within its ring of trees, the old station building stands beyond the village at the end of a long cobbled road. Part is now used as a private house, but the ticket office and waiting room survive – complete with echoing floorboards and potbellied stove. A yellowing timetable curls off a wall. As the train approaches, one or two figures appear on the previously empty platform.

Beyond Rostarzewo, the line becomes thickly wooded and the level crossings apparent only from the warning boards placed just metres in front of them. The shrieking whistle, which is liberally sounded on this part of the journey, bounces off the forest canopy, scattering deer in all directions. Unmanned halts loom out of the darkness, lit by the first rays of dawn. As the train judders to a stop at a wayside station, passengers emerge from the trees carrying panniers of freshly picked mushrooms.

At intervals, freight lines peel off and plunge deep into the forest. One swings south towards Konotop near the German border. Until recently, wagonloads of timber and cement were regularly collected from these lines by German-style Ty42 2-10-0 *kriegsloks*, light freight locomotives built just after World War II for heavy duty on branch lines. But the railway through to Konotop conceals a darker secret, now largely forgotten. Some say this was the line by which trains entered Poland en route to the death camps at Auschwitz and Treblinka. All traces of this anguish have now been obliterated, although an eerie silence remains.

A more lasting reminder of the war, and a sign of the strategic importance of the Berlin–Warsaw axis, lies to the west of Wolsztyn. Snaking down through the forests and fields of the Wielkopolska is the jagged line of the Oder fortifications, built by the Germans in the 1930s to close the defensive corridor between the Oder and Warthe rivers. It was second only to the Maginot Line in strength, and for four months in 1945 kept the Red Army from the gates of Berlin. Above ground, a string of pillboxes and gun emplacements litter the countryside. In the caverns beneath lie miles of tunnels and redoubts, many unexplored since the war. They were kept supplied by a spider's web of narrow gauge tracks that surface deep in the woods. Now destroyed, they once fed into the network that serves Wolsztyn, Poznan and Leszno.

By the time the train reaches the hamlet of Ruchocice the sun has risen and the countryside has opened out to reveal orchards and poppy fields. Much of the track

LEFT *A silver skein of frozen telegraph wires laces the forests between Tloki and Rostarzewo, contrasting dramatically with the billowing smoke from an Ol49.*

ABOVE *At the crossing gate at Szreniawa, cyclists wait for an Ol49 pulling a double-decker passenger train from Poznan to Wolsztyn.*

OPPOSITE *A train from Wolsztyn steams into Poznan, Poland's second largest city. Before 1945, the city was known as Posen.*

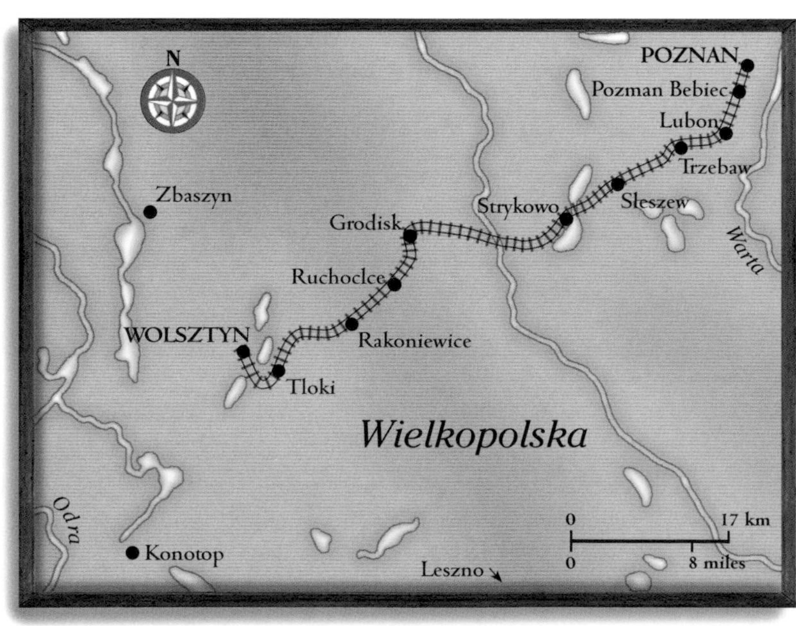

here is overgrown, and tall grass brushes the engine's belly as it slows to take in one of the many speed restrictions. Sunken trackbeds and distorted rails are a perennial hazard along this part of the permanent way, but the momentary slowdown in pace allows passengers to appreciate the wild strawberries and overhanging white laburnum growing alongside the line.

The train speeds up again at Grodzisk, the only sizeable town between Wolsztyn and Poznan. Here the line swerves due east and the sun shines straight into the cab, turning the tracks ahead into arrows of blinding gold. Another freight line veers off to the right, heading toward Koscian in the south. Most of the steam workings here take place during the autumn sugar beet harvest, when two daily services from Wolsztyn exchange wagonloads of coal for an outbound cargo of molasses. Freight shunting in wet weather is a fascinating sight: the lack of an extensive track network necessitates a lot of careful manoeuvring, with the locomotive's driving wheels slipping dramatically under a thousand tons of freight.

Just 24km (15 miles) from Poznan, the water visible on either side of the line at Strykowo and Steszew is part of a skein of lakes that stretch beyond Poznan to Gniezno and Znin in the north, and known as Poland's Little Venice (Wenencja). A favourite weekend retreat for locals, the area has two delightful narrow gauge steam railways. One skirts a small lake, its brightly coloured carriages flitting in and out of the bulrushes. The other is an eccentric, ramshackle affair that begins in the centre of the town of Gniezno and careers toward the countryside on what look like tram tracks. It slews across a series of busy roads before disappearing into the countryside, where it is frequently brought to a halt by errant farmyard animals.

As the train coasts past the back gardens of Lubon just outside Poznan, there is a long-drawn-out whistle from the locomotive – the driver's appreciative greeting to a local beauty. Much of the life of the line resides in its crews, all professional drivers and firemen employed by the state railway. Flamboyant, clever and adept, their ability to combine work and play in a job they love doing is a joy to watch. They communicate on the deafening footplate with cartoon gestures and a slapstick humour shared indiscriminately with passengers, signalmen and crossing-keepers. They remonstrate with reckless drivers, wave at schoolchildren and repair their locomotives on the move, shinning along the boiler to attack a faulty valve with a breathtaking disregard for their own safety. At stations, empty baskets are handed up to the cab and returned full of coal to the grateful stationmistress.

Coming into Poznan, the train passes a shedded Pt47 2-8-2, the third and final class of engine that works the Wolsztyn network, and one that was until recently seen only on this line. Originally built as an international and overnight express, it was once too heavy for the weight restrictions and smaller turntables of the Leszno line, although now it regularly serves most of the network.

Suddenly, a maze of intersecting points and high-voltage wires heralds the approach to Poznan. The carriages have filled up by this point, and although few of the passengers seem to notice that their train is steam-hauled, they are grateful for a regular service in a region where even today levels of car ownership are relatively low, and where distances would otherwise have to be covered by bicycle or even on foot.

Once the last commuters have left the train and disappeared into the bustle of Poland's second-largest city, the engine is uncoupled and runs forward half a mile to the depot, where it is turned, greased and watered for the return journey to Wolsztyn in an hour's time. The inbound run has taken just over two hours, but it is still early, and the smell of fresh coffee and rolls fills the air. As the crew retires in search of breakfast, a few bystanders contemplate the engine's vastness. They may half-realize that tomorrow, or perhaps the next day, the platform will be filled instead with the brashness of a chugging diesel. But just now, they can gaze on a mode of transport that most of us know only from old films or the journeys we make in our imagination. At Wolsztyn, we can, for a time, postpone our final departure from the age of steam.

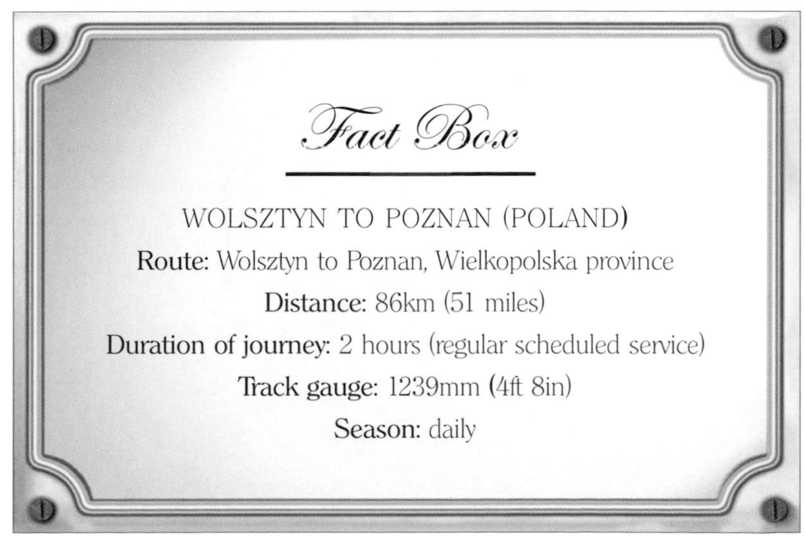

Fact Box

WOLSZTYN TO POZNAN (POLAND)

Route: Wolsztyn to Poznan, Wielkopolska province

Distance: 86km (51 miles)

Duration of journey: 2 hours (regular scheduled service)

Track gauge: 1239mm (4ft 8in)

Season: daily

Sweden

OSTRA SODERMANLANDS JARNVAG

Michael Whitehouse

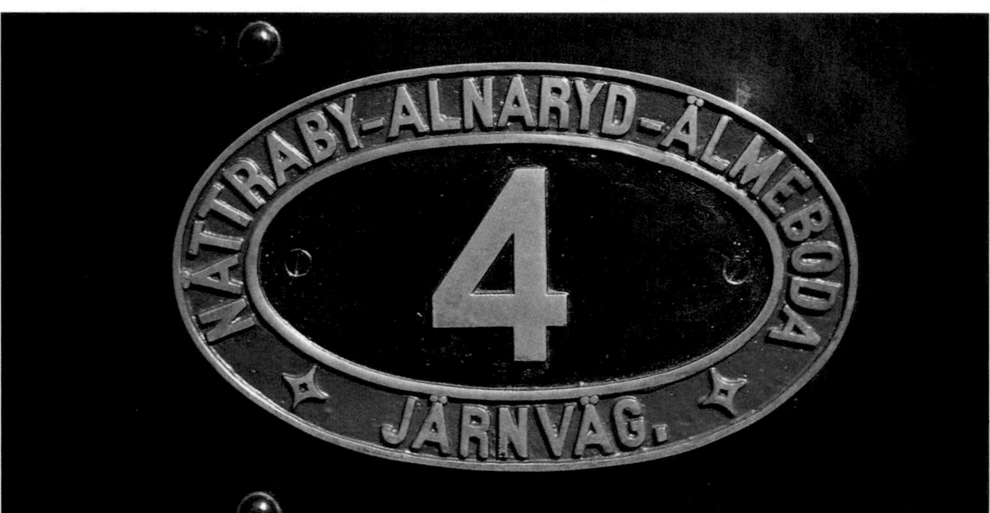

TODAY, NARROW GAUGE STEAM RAILWAYS IN SWEDEN are few and far between. With a view to keeping some of the country's railway heritage operating for tourists, the non-profit Ostra Sodermanlands Jarnvag (OSJ) was formed in 1966. On a former standard gauge branch line, the railway laid two miles of 600mm (1ft 11⅝in) gauge track running from Mariefred, a small town east of Stockholm, to the nearby town of Laggesta. This location was chosen because, for 100 years, Mariefred has been the destination of one of the tourist steamboats plying daily from Stockholm. In fact, it is possible to make the round trip in a day from Stockholm to Mariefred by steamboat, followed by a ride on the narrow gauge steam train to Laggesta and back from there to Stockholm on a high-speed electric train. Our family decided to make this trip, but to take a couple of days to complete it so as to explore the old town and castle at Mariefred.

Capital cities are all about location and Stockholm certainly has one of the best, with beautiful waterfront architecture, a couple of royal palaces and a superb flotilla of steam ferries. We stayed in the Lady Hamilton Hotel, a jewel in the charming old town, promoting a nautical flavour from the moment we stepped into the hotel lobby to be greeted by an old wooden ship's figurehead of a lady adorned in a flowing dress. We walked to the Town Hall quay, where many of the steamboats tie up, to board the

ABOVE *A brass number plate of 2-6-2T* KM Nelsson, *now No. 4 on the roster of the Ostra Sodermanlands Jarnvag.*

RIGHT *Orenstein & Koppel 0-4-4-0T Mallett* Hamra *enters Mariefred station with a morning train from Laggesta.*

5
5

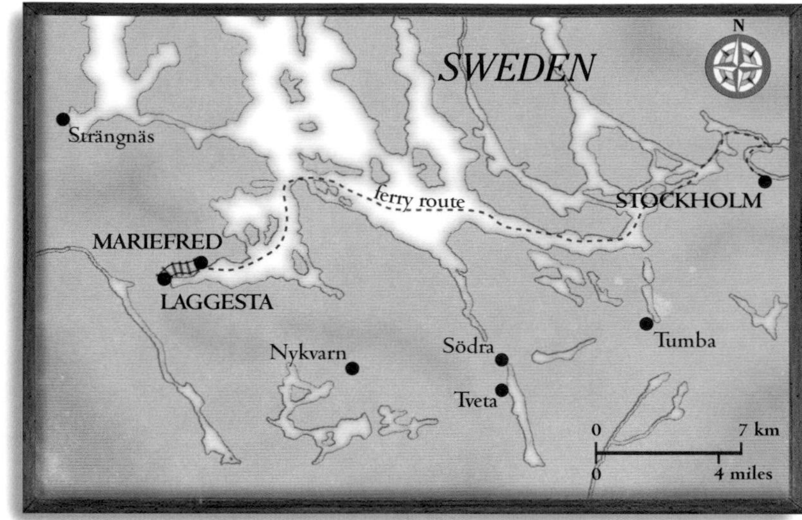

SS *Mariefred* – easy to find as she is the only one with a black funnel. We secured seats on the wooden transverse benches in the warm cabin at the stern for the three-hour sailing up the sea inlet to Mariefred.

The *Mariefred* is a coal-fired steamboat built in 1903 for the non-stop journey to Mariefred. The vessel is still operated by the same company, Gripsholms Mariefred Angfart Gasb, and still uses the same steam engine: a 295-horsepower compound capable of 10 knots per hour.

BELOW *Mariefred station has been adapted from its original standard gauge branch line and is used to serve the tourist needs of the OSJ.*

BELOW RIGHT Hamra *waits in Mariefred station, ready for the 15-minute journey to Laggesta, where passengers can transfer to main line services.*

We left on time at 10am. A crew member in regulation blue woollen pullover untied the mooring ropes and pushed away the gangplank. The captain, wearing his peaked cap, blew three blasts on the ship's hooter and still managed to grin at the noise, although he hears it every day. He relayed instructions to the engine crew down below by means of remote-control brass levers. The ship glided out backwards from the quay, circled round and headed almost silently off to Mariefred, with the outskirts of Stockholm gradually yielding to tree-covered, sparsely populated countryside.

We were allowed into the engine room by climbing the ladder down into the hull. The children's eyes widened when they stood at the porthole just above the waterline and realised they were standing below the surface of the sea. The fireman put a few rounds of coal in the double fireboxes. The engines are capable of 125 revolutions a minute and one has a condenser to convert sea water for use by the boiler. We stood and watched the engines' motion for a few minutes, taking in the aroma of steam and hot oil.

The *Mariefred* arrived at its destination at 1.30pm, where the train was waiting on the short branch line that runs from the town station to the jetty. The string of brown, red and blue coaches was headed by a well-kept, black 0-4-4-0T Mallett, *Hamra*, built by the German manufacturer Orenstein & Koppel in 1902.

We took the train ride to Laggesta (at the other end of the 3.2km/2-mile line) and back straight away, before looking round Mariefred. On the train we sat in a narrow, but delightfully presented second-class coach with wood-panelled interior and were allowed to ride on the end balcony, which was fun as we could more easily hear the rhythmic beat of the engine's exhaust. We had primed our children to present our tickets to the guard. He solemnly clipped them and, with a smile, gave each child his own ticket back.

We looked out of the window at the scenery as we passed historic Gripsholm Castle, the sea inlet and the deer grazing in the open fields beside the passing loop. At Laggesta, *Hamra* ran round the train to prepare for the return journey. Most passengers walked up the path to catch the Stockholm-bound electrified

service at the main-line railway station, but we opted to return to Mariefred with *Hamra* for a look round the town.

Mariefred station is clean and well presented, with a delightful yellow-painted wooden building dating back to the line's standard gauge origins, but it doesn't look out of place on the new railway. The lady in the café took a shine to us when she found we were English and she gave the children posters of some English engines which were displayed on the wall. One was of a special train at Barmouth in Wales taken in the 1960s featuring the Great Western Railway tank engine No. 4555. When I told her that my father had bought this engine for preservation in Devon, she showered copies of this poster on us. I think we could have had the entire stock!

We stayed at the Gripsholm Vardshus Hotel, one of the very oldest hotels in Sweden, which occupies a former monastery built in 1623. The hotel faces the waterfront and is surrounded by picturesque wooden houses – characteristic of the old town – with the whole dominated by a red-spired church. The key feature of Mariefred is Gripsholm Castle, built in the 1530s in red brick with circular domed towers. The castle stands right by the waterfront in an idyllic position only a few minutes' walk from the railway station. There is plenty of time to look round the old town and the castle in the morning, have lunch and take the train back to Laggesta and on to Stockholm.

In the morning, we walked up to the engine shed and yard next to the station. *Hamra* was already in steam, shunting coaches for the day's train. Seeing a railway getting ready for the day's events is always interesting, and we became engrossed by all the activity. For fun, the railway decided to add some freight wagons to the passenger train for a mixed formation. So we happily stood, watched and took photographs. One of the shunters gave hand signals to the engine driver to indicate the next steps, but he forgot to take the handbrake off the tank wagon as it was moved along, so its wheels slid rather than revolved along the track until he noticed his error. The driver saw I had noticed the mistake and we both grinned.

The engine shed is next to the station and houses several tank engines collected from narrow gauge railways all over Sweden. A 2-6-2T No. 4 *KM Nelsson*

Fact Box

OSTRA SODERMANLANDS JARNVAG (SWEDEN)

Route: Mariefred to Laggesta, Södermanlands province

Distance: 3.2km (2 miles)

Duration of journey: 15 minutes (40 minutes return)

Track gauge: 600mm (1ft 11$\frac{5}{8}$in)

Season: Saturdays and Sundays from May to October (daily from 14 June to 25 August)

sat outside raising steam. Inside was *Vira*, a small 2-4-2T over a century old and featuring the distinctive but unusual spark arrestor balloon on the bottom of the chimney, an arrangement that is unique to Sweden.

In summer there are a dozen return steam trips from Mariefred to Laggesta, so there were plenty of trains to choose from for the return journey. At Laggesta, we caught our electric train back to Stockholm. While this high-speed service is efficiently run by the state railway, it lacks the delightful character of the narrow gauge.

BELOW *Gripsholm Castle, built of red brick and featuring distinctive domed towers, is the major landmark of Mariefred.*

BELOW LEFT *The coal-fired steamboat SS* Mariefred *has made the journey from Stockholm to Mariefred daily for more than 100 years.*

Norway

THE SETESDALSBANEN

Colin Boocock

NORWAY IS A COUNTRY OF MOUNTAINS, VALLEYS, PINE FORESTS, LAKES and deep fjords. Some high ground is surmounted by the green-white ice of glaciers which continuously feeds the streams and rivers that, over the ages, have worn down the lower regions into a network of sinuous valleys. Today, the country's road and rail communication links follow these valleys.

Because of the winding nature of the valleys, early railways in southern Norway had to adopt a narrow gauge that was better suited to sharply curved routes and also cheaper to build, and some of these lines live on in preservation today. Nowhere else in the world can you find locomotives like those that work the Setesdalsbanen (Setes Valley Railway) of southern Norway. The 1067mm (3ft 6in) gauge 2-6-2T and 2-4-2T locomotives that work the valley were built specifically for the line, between 1894 and 1902. The four ancient engines that survive out of the original seven are of types unique to the Setesdalsbanen.

This railway is one of Norway's finest preserved lines and offers an accurate representation of what the country's early railways were really like. The Setesdalsbanen was opened in 1896 as a 3ft 6in gauge

ABOVE *The driver lavishes tender loving care on the gleaming workings of this gorgeous 2-6-2T engine, built in Glasgow by Dübs.*

RIGHT *The Setesdalsbanen's operational Norway-built engine, 2-4-2T No. 6, built by Thunes in Kristiana (now Oslo), shows off its big spark arrestor-chimney as it leaves Grovane with two delightful wooden carriages.*

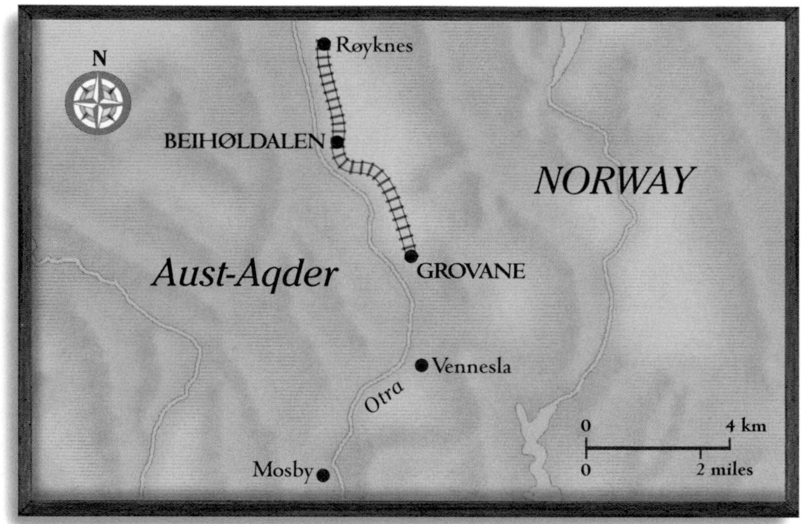

single-track route to connect the inland town of Byglandsfjord and the industries, farms and people of the Setesdal (Setes Valley) with the North Sea port of Kristiansand. The 78km (49-mile) railway thus opened up this relatively isolated area to national and international trade and commerce. It remained an isolated route until construction of the national railway system reached the area, even though the early narrow gauge railways scattered throughout the country totalled around 1300km (800 miles). In 1938 the southern end of the Setesdalsbanen was subsumed into the main railway line from Stavanger and Kristiansand to Oslo and was converted to standard gauge (1435mm/4ft 8½in). That left the inland part of the Byglandsfjord line as an isolated narrow gauge railway from the 'junction' station at Grovane. Diesel railcars were introduced in an attempt to cut the costs of carrying passengers. However, the bother and expense of transferring people and goods between trains at the joint station at Grovane became unrealistic for NSB (Norges Statsbaner – Norwegian State Railways) and so the narrow gauge line was closed in 1962. NSB's last narrow gauge line had gone, or so it seemed.

Thankfully, it was the efforts of a group of railway enthusiasts that persuaded NSB to defer selling or scrapping the assets of the line until an arrangement could be made to secure its future. Train workings were partly reactivated in 1964, from when the line has grown to become the successful operation it is today. Traversing a most attractive valley and surrounded by forests and scenic splendour, the Setesdalsbanen is surely Norway's best steam railway.

The current timetable has three return workings on every Sunday between mid-June and the end of August. These leave Grovane station at 11.30am, 1.00pm and 2.30pm for a return journey lasting less than an hour. There is also a steam train each Tuesday to Friday evening in late July starting from Grovane at 6.00pm. On other weeks in July the evening service is a heritage diesel railcar. This unit also works a Thursday midday service throughout July.

The railway's unique charm stems from the fact that its original locomotives are used for the steam-hauled trains. The oldest are Nos. 1 and 2 which came from the Dübs factory in Glasgow, Scotland, in 1894. These are 2-6-2Ts which carry a combination of Dübs's own British features as well as some specifically Scandinavian design traits. The smokebox door hinges, which end in a ring round the centre of the door, are a decorative feature typical of this manufacturer. You can also see this

on preserved locomotives in other countries, such as Spain. On the other hand, the large, enclosed cab is sensibly Scandinavian, being designed to protect the crew from bitter winter weather. The locomotives have two domes atop their boilers: the brass-trimmed one is the steam collector, and the more mundane painted dome covers the sandbox. (Sand sometimes has to be scattered on the rails in front of the driving wheels to stop the engine from slipping when starting on wet rails.) One prominent item is the large angular spark arrestor that surrounds the chimney. This is clearly needed in such a densely wooded area, where a spark or a speck of burning fuel could easily ignite a serious forest fire.

The Setesdalsbanen also had some similar 2-6-2Ts and some larger-wheeled 2-4-2Ts supplied by the Thunes factory of what is now Oslo, but which is described on the locomotive builder's plates as the city of Kristiana (Oslo's former name). One of the 2-4-2Ts survives in preservation as the railway's locomotive No. 6.

Fact Box

SETESDALSBANEN (NORWAY)
Route: Grovane to Røyknes, Aust-Agder province
Distance: 8km (5 miles)
Duration of journey: 1 hr round trip; up to three return trips (Sundays)
Track gauge: 1067mm (3ft 6in)
Season: Sundays from mid-June to end August

LEFT *The afternoon steam train meanders along the beautiful Setes Valley amid conifer-covered slopes and in sight of high mountains.*

The seven restored carriages used by the Setesdalsbanen today are typical Norwegian timber-sided vehicles, their varnished, slatted sides suggesting an early stage in railway development. Indeed most were originally built by the Skabo company in the late 19th century, though not for the line to Byglandsfjord. They have been rebuilt during their long lives, and have been acquired for service in the Setesdal. They make very satisfactory companions for the classic steam tank engines used on this line. There is also a fleet of 18 freight wagons, the oldest dating from 1881 and the latest from 1944. Lastly, there are two diesel railcars and a pair of former NSB shunting tractors of Class Skd 206.

We join the train at the station at Grovane. This is situated adjacent to the main line station on the NSB Stavanger–Kristiansand–Oslo route, but as NSB has not yet seen fit to reopen their part of the station there are regrettably no connections with NSB trains here. The bus service in this part of the country is also very limited, so to reach the Setesdalsbanen visitors must travel to Grovane by car. Here you can see 2-6-2T No. 1 displayed on a plinth, a fitting reminder to passers-by that there is an historic railway here.

Our steam locomotive has a parcels and guard's van behind it, followed by the passenger carriages, the whole arrangement looking a true period piece. We can observe that the track is lightly laid with relatively small-section flat-bottom rails, which makes the gauge appear broader than its nominal 1067mm (3ft 6in). After a slow start, the train passes the locomotive and rolling stock sheds on the left. We call at the single-platform station that was the preserved railway's starting point before the company reopened its platform alongside the NSB line at the start of the 21st century. Our engine now opens up for a period of steep gradient climbing. The 2-6-2T is master of its load. We traverse a winding track past stands of coniferous trees, the train climbing along a narrowing valley through a rock cutting. Sometimes the track is set on a ledge above the small River Otra. We cross over a long bridge of lattice-girder construction and the engine chatters through a lengthy stretch of pine forest before passing a high dam at the southern end of a long reservoir, the Byglandsfjorden. The track then skirts the reservoir until it reaches Beihøldalen. Then the train passes onto the newest part of the railway, which was reopened in 2004, and terminates at the village of Røyknes. We have travelled 8km (5 miles) on this beautiful line and have enjoyed lovely mountain views on the upper part. The railway cannot reach Byglandsfjord any more: there has been too much modern development across the track bed.

When you visit this charming railway, park your car at Grovane and spend some time looking around the depot before joining your train for the twisting climb up the valley. Listen to the pulse of the exhaust from the old engine's long chimney, and imagine you are back in the 19th century. Smoke from wood fires rises from the chimneys of the wooden houses in the villages. Perhaps the rain is still dripping from the conifers, there is the splash and whisper of the small river and even smaller valley-side streams. Here you can soak up the atmosphere of old Norway in more ways than one!

Africa

Eritrea

RAILWAY REVIVAL IN THE HORN OF AFRICA

Nick Lera

RISEN FROM THE ASHES OF WAR, the railway they said could never be rebuilt has staged a dramatic comeback. The young country of Eritrea in the Horn of Africa has achieved the seemingly impossible and put together the shattered remnants of its old Italian colonial railway to provide the 21st-century traveller with one of the most outstanding mountain train rides available in the world today. Along with the famous lines that conquered the Andes, the Alps, the Rockies and the Himalayas, this revival in Africa's Great Rift Valley has now regained its rightful place as one of the railway wonders of the world. What's more, the trip can be enjoyed with the line's original steam locomotives, of which no less than three have been restored. These sturdy machines steam confidently round hairpin bends, plunging in and out of long tunnels and ravines, often clinging to the mountainside with a sheer 305m (1000ft) drop below, mostly on a constant gradient of 1 in 28.

ABOVE *Over the years, Eritrea's railways have seen Italian, British and Ethiopian control. This driver now works for the Eritrean government.*

RIGHT *A classic Italian colonial train from the 1930s waits to depart from the Red Sea port of Massawa.*

PREVIOUS PAGES *The Outeniqua Choo-Tjoe steams across the bridge over Knysna Lagoon on South Africa's Garden Route.*

The restored part of Eritrea's railway, originally dubbed 'the steel snake', is 117.6km (73 miles) in length. It starts at the port of Massawa on the Red Sea and ends in the capital, Asmara, at an elevation of 2342m (7683ft). The history of this remarkable railway is to some extent the history of the country itself, as it was essential to the establishment of the colony and the creation of its mountain capital, formerly just a village at a crossroads.

The Italians arrived in the Red Sea during the 1870s, and steadily acquired coastal enclaves from Assab up towards Massawa, which was occupied in 1885. Construction of a railway began in 1887, but territorial disputes with the Ethiopians, involving several major battles, caused years of delay. It was not until 1904 that the line into the hills reached Ghinda, at kilometre 69. At an elevation of 888m (2913ft) the temperate climate here was a welcome relief from the baking heat of the coast. It was well suited for a railway headquarters, and for the next seven years Ghinda remained the terminus and railhead for further construction towards Asmara.

It is the 45km (28 mile) section above Ghinda, climbing 1506m (4940ft) to the Asmara summit, at 2394m (7854ft) above sea level, that constitutes the engineering miracle of the Eritrean Railways. Even by today's standards, its completion in only seven years would be impressive. The ruling gradient of 1 in 28, or 3.5 per cent, never varies throughout, a vital factor ensuring consistent locomotive performance up grade, and steady conditions for the essential business of controlling the brakes on the descent. There are seven major viaducts, no less than 22 tunnels, and several large retaining walls, all perfectly engineered and elegantly finished in faced stonework. The twists and turns of this section can best be judged by comparing the distance as the crow flies of 20km (12½ miles) with the 45km (28-mile) track length.

When the railway finally reached Asmara, 2km (1¼ miles) beyond the summit at 117.6km (73 miles) from the coast, in 1911, it provided the spur for the creation of a model Italian city in the heart of Africa. When Fascist leader Benito Mussolini (1883–1945) came to power in 1922, he decided that Eritrea should become the showpiece of his new Roman Empire, so he encouraged Italian immigration and poured resources into Asmara. Broad avenues were laid out, with a governor's residence and a Roman Catholic cathedral. The population grew steadily, encouraged by the prosperity of the new colony, and by the 1930s an astonishing Modernist city had taken shape, complete with stylish Art Deco architecture (which survives today). At this time, too, the railway workshops and headquarters were moved up from Ghinda and work started on a 188km (117-mile) extension to Agordat in the west of the colony, which opened in 1922. A further extension to the Sudan border was started but never completed.

But there was another agenda: Eritrea was to serve as the springboard for Italy's long-planned invasion of Ethiopia (or Abyssinia, as it was then known),

LEFT *En route to Ghinda with a passenger special from Massawa, a pair of Italian Mallet-type locos skirt the edge of the great Danakil Depression – one of the hottest places on earth – at Moncullo.*

BELOW *Rahel prepares coffee among the slatted wooden seats of a 1912-vintage Italian-built carriage.*

which finally took place in 1935. The Italian army took control of the railway, and traffic peaked between March and October of that year when the Abyssinian War reached its height. No less than 34 locomotives were shipped out in 1936–38, to relieve the by now exhausted original stock, and 11 new railcars also appeared, one of them fitted out as an ambulance to rush battlefield casualties down to hospital ships in Massawa.

But in the end little was achieved by all this build-up. After Italy entered World War II on Hitler's side, Eritrea found itself with a hostile neighbour in the form of British-controlled Sudan. A British force, which included Indian, East African and South African troops, invaded the country early in 1941, and a two month campaign ensued. The Italians made a stand in the Keren Gorge but their resistance faltered following the death in action of their commander, General Lorenzini, on 17 March. Keren fell 10 days later and Asmara was taken on 1 April. The Second Roman Empire was over.

Eritrea then came under British military administration; traffic was made to drive on the left, English-language road signs went up, and the *Eritrea Daily Bulletin* and *Eritrea News and Sportsman* appeared on newsstands in the capital. In their caretaker role, the British maintained and even improved the railway. A new branch line was laid to an Agip oil depot, badly worn track was renewed, and part of the mountain cut away at kilometre 107 to eliminate a troublesome S-bend.

However, the railway increasingly came under attack from the *shifta*, political bandits backed by Ethiopia. Favourite targets were the Fiat *littorina* railcars, which carried the first-class (and hence mainly European) passengers. Wire cages were fitted over the carriage roofs so that grenades would bounce off out of harm's way. In one incident, a grenade rebounded off a rock cutting and blew a large hole in the side of a railcar. Luckily nobody was hurt.

In 1952, under UN auspices, the country was federated with Ethiopia. The British left, and Eritrea was airbrushed off the map of Africa. The people of Eritrea felt betrayed because they believed they had a strong case for independence. The seeds of resistance were sown. After 1974, when Colonel Mengistu seized power in Ethiopia, establishing a Marxist regime backed by the Soviet Union, Eritrean resistance broke out into a full-scale war of independence.

A major casualty in the conflict was the railway which, being in government hands, was subjected to continual acts of sabotage by the Eritrean People's Liberation Front (EPLF). The last train to Asmara ran in December 1975, when a steam locomotive arrived pulling 15 empty wagons. The train had left Massawa with a load of stores for the Ethiopian army but en route the EPLF cleared it of its contents at the isolated station of Baresa. With an eye to the future, the Eritrean fighters' adopted a strategy of not damaging the railway itself but rather attempting, through continual harrassment, to render it unusable by the Ethiopian

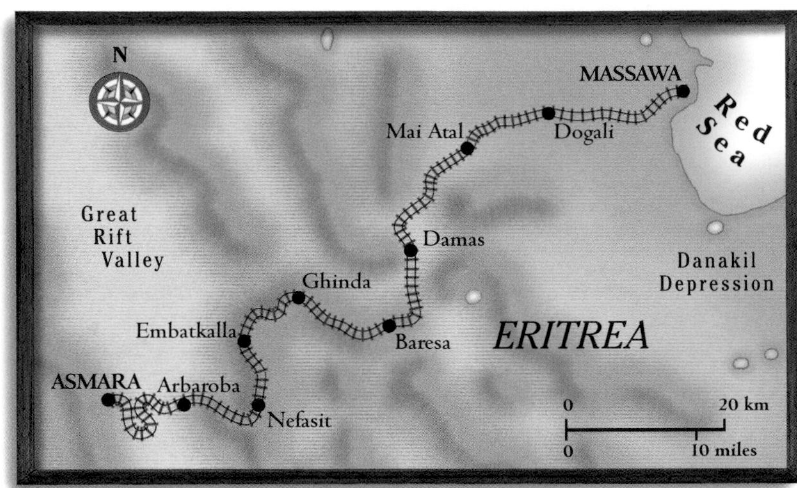

government forces. The major bridges were mined, with skull and crossbone warning signs boldly displayed to discourage the Ethiopians from using the line. Most of the track was ripped up by both sides to build bunkers. Tunnels and cuttings were blocked, and a bridge over the Massawa highway blown up by the Ethiopians to allow tank transporters to pass. But, as planned, the rest of the railway's infrastructure was unharmed.

From their famous 'bunker city' at Nakfa in the northern hills, the EPLF fighters waged an incredibly brave and tough war involving much sacrifice and hardship, eventually exhausting the Ethiopians, who were expelled in 1991. The conflict had been kept away from the capital, so it was from an almost undamaged Asmara that Eritrea's triumphant declaration of independence was made.

But the unexpected often seems to happen in Africa, and war-ravaged Eritrea was no exception. In 1994, to everyone's amazement and the delight of railfans, the government announced it was going to rebuild the railway. This was initially a political decision rather than an economic one. The 'steel snake' that originally formed the backbone of the country was seen as an important symbol of nationhood, setting Eritrea apart from its departed overlord, Ethiopia. The latest plan is to continue the reconstruction westwards to facilitate trade with Sudan.

But the Eritreans faced a truly monumental task. US and Italian consultants variously estimated the cost of reconstruction at between US$100 million and US$400 million, but this was far more than the government could afford. But rather than abandon the project, they resorted to self-help. Local road hauliers were asked to carry railway materials whenever trucks were returning empty; army conscripts were drafted in to clear blocked tunnels and trained to lay track; and scores of veteran railwaymen came out of retirement to instruct and advise. Some of the track was missing, but teams of volunteers located most of it by scouring the battle zones for abandoned rails in trenches and bunkers. Only the clips and fishplates had to be imported. It took seven years to finish the job, at a cost of just five per cent of the lowest original estimate.

My first visit to Eritrea coincided with the final phase of the reconstruction in 2002. I was received by Amanuel Ghebreselassie, the general manager, who invited me to inspect the works at Nefasit (24km/15 miles from Asmara). This involved a bone-shattering ride on a wagon hauled by a captured Ethiopian truck of the Soviet 'Ural' type, which had been modified to run on rails. It took me from

LEFT *Two Italian Mallets (built 1915 and 1938, respectively) flank a 202 shunting engine at Asmara's railway workshops.*

OPPOSITE, BELOW *The imposing campanile of Asmara's Romanesque-style cathedral is a reminder of the Italian origin of Eritrea's capital.*

BELOW *Ninety-four-year-old Negash holds one of the wooden forms used to produce the moulds required for casting replacement parts.*

Nefasit, dominated by a high peak surmounted by the ancient Debre Bizen Monastery, down the edge of the escarpment towards Embatkalla. We were taking ballast down to the railhead where teams of soldiers pounced on the wagons and tipped out five tons in as many minutes. As the Ural pulled away to fetch another load, the men were already shovelling the ballast under newly laid rails and bedding in the sleepers (crossties).

With a loud squeal the brake was briefly released as a work camp on rails slowly crept down the mountain behind the tracklayers. Female railway clerks in colourful garb sat on a flatcar doling out bolts and fixing-screws with large tin mugs into head baskets carried by waiting soldiers. Once bolted together, the rails had to be forced into position with crowbars to fit the curvature of the trackbed. But just a few metres further on the curve was so sharp that it took more than a crowbar to bend the rails. An ancient device from the early days of railways was then brought into use. The *gira rotaia* (Italian for 'rail-bender') consists of an adjustable set of pinch rollers through which the rail is forced by a rotating spindle pushed by four men with two-metre bars who dance round the contraption like an ancient treadmill. Primitive but effective, it bends a 10m (33ft) rail in about three minutes.

Back in Asmara, the railway yards which had been disused for 25 years were coming back to life. Being prepared for its first steam test was newly restored locomotive No. 442-055, the very same one that had hauled the last train up from Baresa in December 1975. Built in Italy in 1938, it was an imposing articulated machine of the Mallet type. A team of elderly fitters, mostly over 70 years of age, were climbing all over the engine, adjusting the safety valve, checking pistons and brakes, oiling the bearings and cleaning the connecting rods. The clock had really been turned back for these men and they were obviously enjoying every minute of it. In charge was the imposing figure of the depot chief, 78-year-old Sium Beraki, who wore a long green cotton coat, the classic attire of the senior artisan of old. He had joined the railway in 1940, aged 16, working his way up through cleaner, fireman and driver to loco foreman – as high as a 'native' could be promoted in colonial times. In precise Italian, he pointed out the locomotive's *doppia espansione* (double expansion) compound system, which re-uses the exhaust steam to power a second set of cylinders.

With a toot of its whistle, a tiny four-wheel shunting loco announced it was ready to take me up a short branch line to the revived railway workshops. A steam hammer was thumping away in the foundry, while in an adjoining workshop I was introduced to the leading contender for the title of world's oldest railwayman: 94-year-old Negash, who works as a pattern-maker. He had served as a soldier in the Italian Army in the 1930s (an 'askari', as they were known) and joined the railway in 1942 under

the British. He proudly showed us rack upon rack stuffed with the smooth, red-painted wooden forms he had made over the last 60 years. For every part of a locomotive or wagon that needed to be cast, Negash had a pattern to make the mould. Bright-eyed and alert, he claimed the key to his longevity was a good woman.

My next visit to Eritrea was in 2003 to see the completed railway and to make a film of those marvellous Italian compound engines at work. I joined a 40-strong tour group drawn from all over the world – Italians (of course), British, Germans, Dutch and even Japanese. Having flown into Asmara, we started the journey with a nail-biting descent by bus of the endless hairpin bends on the road down to Massawa. The stunning views en route are punctuated by glimpses of rusting tanks and other armoured vehicles dotting the hills. A railway viaduct would briefly appear beside us and then be gone, the line suddenly reappearing in a distant loop far below. From the road it is hard to conceive how it might be possible to build a railway in such terrain.

Located on the northern edge of the great Danakil Depression, Massawa enjoys a temperature of 38°C (100°F) and high humidity in the cool season. The hot season is not recommended. The ravages of years of war have robbed Massawa of its one-time status as the 'Pearl of the Red Sea', but life has returned to the old city. There are many interesting Ottoman and Egyptian buildings to be seen, with their enclosed carved wooden balconies, and a few wooden Arab dhows still grace the old harbour.

The terrace of the Dahlak Hotel has a grandstand view of the railway causeway across Massawa's inner harbour, and breakfast taken here while observing the trains rates high on the scale for a steam enthusiast. Several tour companies now offer special steam rail journeys in Eritrea. It is advisable to join one of these as steam is unlikely to be used in regular service – for which diesels are planned.

Our locomotive, No. R442-059, stands proudly on the quayside of Old Massawa as locals peer out curiously from the arcade of the bazaar. Its polished brass plates gleaming in the morning sun provide an instant history lesson. The prefix R stands for *ridotto* (reduced or narrow), a reference to the gauge. Built by Ansaldo in Genoa, the date 1938 is suffixed XVI, indicating the 16th year of Fascist rule. 'Acqua 6m^3' gives the water capacity at 6 cu m (212 cu ft), or 6000 litres (1320 gallons), so we shall clearly have to stop for more water along the way. The whistle blows and the driver of our Mallet locomotive cautiously admits steam to the high-pressure cylinder under the cab. As the engine starts to move, a second whoosh of steam is heard as the big cylinders in front receive the exhaust flow and start to pull in their turn. The extra surge of power can be felt straightaway on the bare benches of our antique third-class wooden carriage, built in Milan in 1912. (Regrettably the first-class ones were destroyed during the war.) Every joint in the rails can be felt just as clearly, too; before the advent of the railcars, the 10-hour journey to Asmara must have been a trip to remember. But our ride is in easy stages over two days, with plenty of refreshment stops, and any mild discomforts are overshadowed by anticipation of the exciting journey ahead.

We whistle through modern Massawa on the mainland, where everyone turns out to wave, and head off across almost empty semi-desert, observed by a few camels chewing pensively at the green shoots of razor-sharp thorn trees, which miraculously cause them no harm. On the approach to Dogali we pause to photograph our vintage train crossing a graceful 14-arch bridge over a dry riverbed, then pass a small hill topped by an Italian monument to the 500 soldiers who fell in a battle with the Ethiopians here in 1887. We make our first water stop on the edge of the desert at Mai Atal, picking our way with cameras past a rusty, overturned wagon, its wheels in the air. The weirdly bent rails around the shell hole next to it tell their own story.

Soon we are under way again and the steady beat of the loco can be heard as we start to climb into the foothills on the 40km (25-mile) stretch of the line to Ghinda that diverges from the main road. After crossing an elegant single-arch stone bridge we come to the village of Damas, with its small white mosque by the track. Villagers with their camels and conscripts from a nearby army camp gather round to see the unusual trainload of foreigners, while the locomotive receives coal from an army truck.

Beyond Damas not even a truck can penetrate. The line follows a long dry riverbed where a camel train can be seen picking its way between the stones. Suddenly there is a frantic whistling from the locomotive. Our brake men hurriedly screw down the handwheels on the carriage balconies to bring the train grinding to a halt. A 'shifta' attack, perhaps? Not quite; unused to the mechanical competition about to threaten his livelihood, a herdsman with another camel train has led his animals right into the path of our locomotive. When the panic subsides much laughter ensues and a nicely posed photograph is arranged.

This portion of the journey, with no roads, towns or even villages nearby, shows us the challenge faced by the Italians in 1890 when they started to survey the railway. We storm across a splendid five-arch viaduct – one of several – and think of how every brick and stone used to build it had to be brought up on camel-back. A lunch stop at the oasis of Baresa means more water for the engine, and a picnic for our group in the ruins of the old station, whose slender, cast-iron Ionic columns no longer have a roof to support. In faded paint on the wall the height is lettered in feet as well as metres (1968ft/600m), a reminder of the British presence in the 1940s.

As we continue towards Ghinda, green patches begin to appear in the riverbed, and we see donkeys grazing. The cooler air is a relief as we leave the heat of the coast behind. Our hard-working locomotive steams into newly rebuilt Ghinda station, and our first day's trip is over. But before we rejoin our tour bus, an excellent photo call is arranged, with two of the 1938 Mallets and two of the small 0-4-0 shunting engines – all four of them in steam – proudly lined up for our cameras. Not bad for a railway that was closed and lifted 25 years earlier.

But the next day is the one we have all been waiting for. We return to Ghinda and reboard our 1912 carriage, where the charming Rahel, the general manager's secretary and acting catering supervisor for the day, takes freshly roasted coffee beans off her Primus stove and hands round samples for her guests to savour the aroma before the coffee is brewed. The unlikely setting for this traditional local ceremony sets the tone for a very special day indeed, as we set off on the most spectacular part of the railway.

OPPOSITE *Above Baresa the line climbs out of the river valley towards Ghinda over a typical example of Eritrea's well-engineered viaducts.*

RIGHT *The final stage of the climb to Asmara takes the train squealing round this tight curve above a sheer 300m (984ft) drop at Devil's Gate, just before the summit at 2394m (7854ft) above sea level.*

ABOVE *Traffic manager Techlias Mendar supervises Eritrean army conscripts re-laying track as part of the reconstruction of the railway near Embatkalla at the foot of the Rift Valley escarpment.*

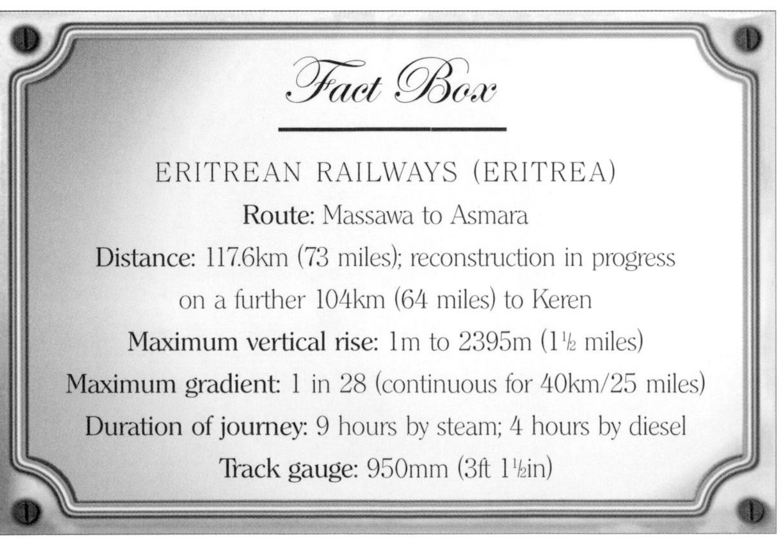

Fact Box

ERITREAN RAILWAYS (ERITREA)

Route: Massawa to Asmara

Distance: 117.6km (73 miles); reconstruction in progress on a further 104km (64 miles) to Keren

Maximum vertical rise: 1m to 2395m (1½ miles)

Maximum gradient: 1 in 28 (continuous for 40km/25 miles)

Duration of journey: 9 hours by steam; 4 hours by diesel

Track gauge: 950mm (3ft 1½in)

The locomotive is worked hard from the start. The gradient is a continual 1 in 28 (3.5 per cent), and as we roar up the line the green valleys give way to rocky slopes as we ascend the Rift Valley escarpment. But just as the views improve, they begin to fade. The sun disappears, rain drives at the windows and we hastily pull on our jackets against a sudden chill. At an elevation of 1500m (5000ft) we have entered a typical Rift Valley cloud bank. Through the front balcony door, the glow from the locomotive's firebox relieves the gloom inside the carriage as the fireman shovels coal. We slow down and our guide tells us we are entering Nefasit. Through the mist white-robed figures can faintly be seen, and the sound of a hundred ululating women – some bowing, some waving – echoes round the train as it comes to a halt. The people of Nefasit have turned out in force to welcome their first passenger train, and rush up to shake the hands of each and every member of the train crew – a moving sight indeed.

With water tanks topped up, and the crowd still waving, the locomotive heads off, driving blind at full power into the thick fog, whistling continually. We can feel the carriage sway as we go round a tight curve and hear the klaxon of an unseen diesel truck on the road above. The roar of a tunnel then engulfs us, and we come out into the clouds again, but they are thinner now, and we begin to make out the shapes of ravines and distant peaks. The train then plunges into a long straight tunnel,

ABOVE *The 'Steel Snake' coils round yet another spur, halfway up the escarpment section above Nefasit. The driver has obligingly stopped the train for photos at this remote and inaccessible spot.*

and windows fly up as thick smoke begins to fill the carriage. We emerge into bright sunlight to find ourselves literally suspended from the mountainside, and confronted with a spectacular vista of the northern Rift Valley. We are now at 1800m (6000ft), with a sheer drop of 300m (1000ft) to the valley below. Not for the faint-hearted.

When we reach Arbaroba station, a large crowd of villagers with water pots has to be politely asked to stand aside while the legitimate user of the newly restored water supply steams up for a refill. With its Italian nameboard and fretwork canopy, this is the prettiest surviving station, in a superb setting on the edge of the escarpment. There is time to stretch our legs and admire the views framed in the arches of the adjacent stone viaduct. Our train now crosses the viaduct and enters the famous series of four double loops on the final 12km (7½-mile) stretch to Asmara. The curves here are even sharper than before, but we ride into them with scarcely a hint of a lurch thanks to our compound-powered front bogie which pulls the loco smoothly round.

In a typically ingenious piece of engineering, we leave the Durfo valley at kilometre 110 through a tunnel piercing the Rift Valley escarpment, swing round a tight 500m (1640ft) curve on the side of a sheer precipice and then re-enter the valley in a deep cutting just before the Asmara summit at 2394m (7854ft). This stretch was dubbed the Devil's Gate by the line's builders and the name has stuck. The photo stop here, with clouds in the valley far below and towering crags beside the line, provides the defining image of the railway and rounds off the most superb trip imaginable for the lover of steam travel.

At Asmara station we all applaud the general manager and his staff for their Herculean efforts, which have produced the finest steam revival of the 21st century. Relaxing over a Melotti beer before flying home, I have to play back some of the video to convince myself I haven't imagined it all. Long may it last.

Eritrean Railways are now seeking to acquire some modern rolling stock to provide regular passenger and freight service from Asmara to the coast, saving the steam locomotives for tourist charters. Meanwhile reconstruction is now continuing further west to Keren (104km/65 miles from Asmara) and beyond, with the long-term aim of fulfilling the Italians' original plan to create a 450km (280-mile) railway from the Red Sea to the Sudan border. An ambitious project indeed, but judging by the progress made so far it would be unwise to dismiss it as a pipe dream.

South Africa

THE BANANA EXPRESS

Paul Ash

The small toy train climbs up on its narrow gauge from the Umzimkulu valley into the hills. It climbs up to Carisbrooke, and when it stops there, you may get out for a moment and look down on the great valley from which you have come. It is not likely the train will leave you, for there are few people here, and everyone will know who you are... It is interesting to wait for the train at Carisbrooke, while it climbs out of the great valley. Those who know can tell with each whistle where it is, at what road, what farm, what river.

THIS PASSAGE, FROM ALAN PATON'S CELEBRATED NOVEL, *Cry, The Beloved Country* (1948), prepared me for adventures on South Africa's narrow gauge railways. Much of the line Paton described is gone now, torn up and sold for scrap, although the bit that passes through Carisbrooke survives. But 160km (100 miles) to the south, a similar narrow gauge line, owned by the Alfred County Railway (ACR), makes its way up from the subtropical coast and into the green hills of southern KwaZulu-Natal province. From the seaside town of Port Shepstone, the ACR's Banana Express wanders along the beachfront for a few miles, before making a sudden, 90-degree turn and clambering into the hills.

ABOVE *A proud Roelf van Wyngaardt, the Alfred County Railway's 'Uncle Steam', stands on the footplate of a Garratt he has just rebuilt.*

RIGHT *The Banana Express huffs upgrade through lush coastal forest, slipping past stands of the trees from which it takes its name.*

ABOVE *The ACR's magnificent NGG16 Garrat locomotive, No. 155, hauls a train through stands of eucalyptus trees near Paddock, inland terminus of the Banana Express.*

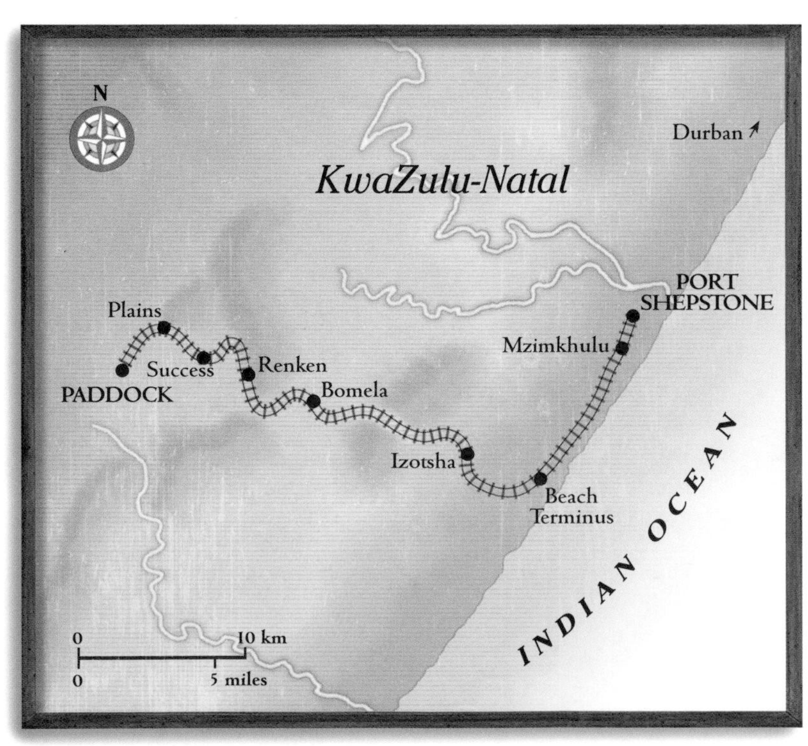

Southern KwaZulu-Natal is a country of hills spawned, if you like, by the Drakensberg Mountains, the 'Barrier of Spears', which run in a jagged line from the northeastern tip of South Africa and down in a rocky arc into the southwest. Dozens of rivers have their headwaters here, falling off the edge of the mountains and heading eastward to the Indian Ocean in great valleys and gorges. At the bottom of the gorges live antelope, baboons, monkeys and reclusive predators such as caracal and even leopard. Few people live next to these tumbling rivers, but on the top of the fertile hills it is different. Zulu homesteads – round, thatched huts with white walls – cluster on the hillsides, surrounded by patches of maize and vegetable plots. Indigenous forest – yellowwood, stinkwood and ironwood trees – grows thickly in the gorges. On top, there are swathes of eucalyptus and wattle plantations, which contribute to the economy of the province.

This is the difficult country crossed by the ACR. The railway was built to serve farmers and timber growers and, like all such narrow gauge lines, it was built as cheaply as possible. To keep costs down, a gauge of 610mm (2ft) was adopted. Any wider and the railway would have been too expensive to construct, such are the hills and deep valleys through which it wanders on its 121km (75-mile) route – with the Banana Express covering a third of this distance – from the sea to the forestry town of Harding. When it was finished, they called it the 'Mae West line' because of its generous curves.

I join the train from Port Shepstone to Paddock on a rainy Saturday. Charlie Lewis, Alfred County Railway managing director, welcomes us aboard: 'We are not in a hurry, so have a good ride.' With a sharp whistle and a woof of steam, the tiny NGG16 Garratt locomotive tugs us out of the station.

Without Charlie Lewis, the railway would have suffered the same fate as the other narrow gauge lines in Natal (as the province was known prior to 1994). In 1986, he and a group of investors bought the line off its then owner, the South African Railways, which was about to shut it down. The lumbering, inefficient SAR said the line was not economical, a no-hoper. There was no traffic, they said, and the only logical thing to do was to close it and tear up the rails. Lewis disagreed. He looked at the sweeping wattle and gum plantations, and spoke to the farmers whose land lay along the line, and saw opportunity there. In 1987, the Alfred County Railway began hauling timber from the forest around Harding, just as it did when trains began running in 1917.

It was tough. The railway, hauling trains on its own tracks, was competing against trucks which were running on roads paid for by the state. The management came up with novel solutions for hauling timber – like loading the logs crossways instead of vertically – that would increase the payload. A couple of articulated Garratt locomotives were rebuilt to incorporate modern steam technology, boosting their power and cutting running costs. But in 2000, floods washed away upper sections of the line and through trains stopped running. It looked like the end.

But Charlie Lewis is blessed with unstoppable determination. With little freight to haul on the lower section of the line, he concentrated on the Banana Express, the passenger excursion train which currently forms the nucleus of the ACR's operations. In October 2003, NGG16 locomotive No. 127 was returned to service. The little Garratt has become the heart of the railway, and its sweet, roaring whistle floating over the hills and valleys tells listeners that the Banana Express is on its way.

Our train rattles out of Port Shepstone and noses into the banana groves. Lewis has marshalled a balcony-end saloon at the back of the train and I commandeer one side of it for the journey, watching the track roll away behind in the shadow of the banana trees, listening to the wheels clacking over the gaps in the unwelded rails. A fellow traveller stands on the balcony with me, gripping the handrail as the wooden coach sways and rolls over the track. 'Is it meant to roll around like this', he asks. The rock-and-roll is one of the joys of narrow gauge rail travel. 'Absolutely', I reply.

To the right we see the Indian Ocean as the banana groves open up briefly. Just as we are lulled into thinking that banana trees are the only scenery, the train rumbles onto the trestle bridge over the Ifafa River. From the coach window, you can see the water 10m (30ft) below. To the south, so close that mist from the breakers settles on your skin, the Indian Ocean roars up onto the beach. Soon afterwards, the line curves sharply inland and the first real climb of the day begins. Doubling back on itself, the line climbs through the banana groves, ducks under the busy N2 highway bridge and clambers towards Izotsha, 13km (8 miles) out of Port Shepstone.

By now, the loco is really working hard to cope with the wet rails and five coaches full of travellers. Clumps of lush grass growing near the rails are ground into a fine paste under the wheels and the Garratt comes slipping to a halt. The driver eases the train back a few feet and then takes another run at the bank. With much slipping and gouts of steam and smoke, and helped by a sander laying a thin trail of grit on the rails, the little Garratt finds her feet and barks up the hill.

After a few more tight curves, the train pulls into Izotsha, 110m (360ft) above sea level. The locomotive uncouples and moves up to the watering column while the passengers disembark to visit Zakhele, a craft centre set up in the old station building to provide poor rural people with the means to earn a living. 'Zakhele', says Charlie, 'means "we make".' He's talking about the centre, with its traditional Zulu crafts, but I'm thinking of the gutsy railway that defies the pressure of the modern world to carry on doing what it has been doing for nearly a century. Charlie points to the coaches. 'That one came from the Otavi Railway in German South West Africa. It's over 100 years old. And this carriage', he says, pointing to a beautiful wooden-bodied coach in smart red-and-white livery, 'we just finished building in our own workshops.'

At the other end of the yard, the loco is having a brew-up. While she slakes her thirst at the watering column, the driver busies himself with the steam-age ritual of oiling around and inspecting the running gear, and the fireman builds up a good fire for the climb ahead. A light rain is falling, droplets fizzing on the boiler. The only sounds are water gurgling into the locomotive's tanks, the ring of the fireman's shovel and the patter of rain on the leaves of a row of tall, old gum trees.

'Kom terug vir 'n koppel', says the guard in Afrikaans. 'Come back to couple.' They have to hurry a bit now, because there are buses waiting at Paddock to take some of the passengers to the nature reserve at Oribi Gorge. The driver eases the Garratt back onto its train and whistles for departure. The passengers board and the driver opens the regulator. From here to the current terminus of the line at Paddock, 26km (16 miles) away – 39km (24 miles) from Port Shepstone – it's solid climbing all the way.

The landscape has changed too. The banana groves have given way to open hill country. Zulu homesteads cluster on the hillsides, and from dozens of doorways a stream of excited children run down to meet us. Steam trains have a remarkable effect on people, especially children. Is it the sight of our little train winding through the landscape that excites them? Or the steam hissing from cylinders, the clanking coupling rods and syncopated cha-cha of the Garratt's exhaust? As the loco crew work the train slowly up the hill, the children start singing 'Shosholoza', a traditional Zulu working song, their sweet clear voices rising above the sound of the huffing Garratt. As they wave us goodbye, I hope that the vision of this train in the hills and the smell of hot oil and coal smoke has the same delirious effect on them that it does on me.

Like many heritage railways, the ACR faces a struggle to maintain financial viability. At time of writing, the future of the Banana Express, and of the ACR as a whole, hung in the balance as a result of a dispute with South Africa's national rail operator. For the moment, though, the little train still traces its route through the eucalyptus plantations and banana groves up into the green hills.

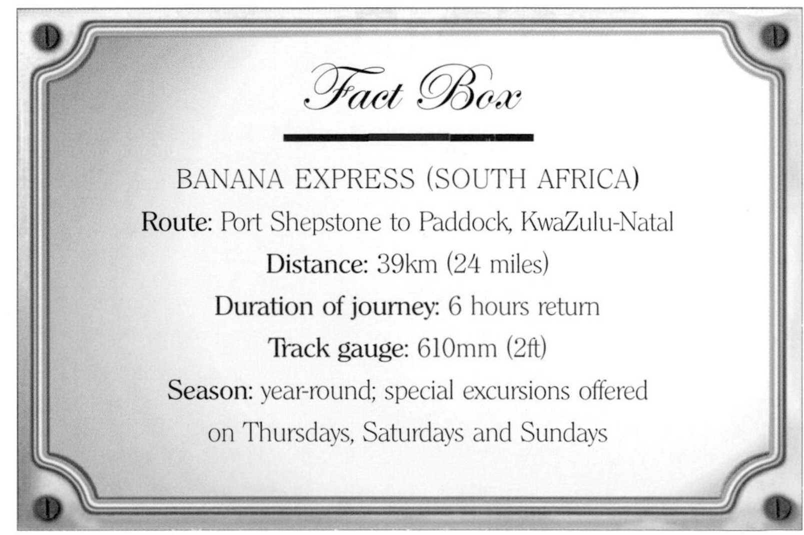

Fact Box

BANANA EXPRESS (SOUTH AFRICA)

Route: Port Shepstone to Paddock, KwaZulu-Natal

Distance: 39km (24 miles)

Duration of journey: 6 hours return

Track gauge: 610mm (2ft)

Season: year-round; special excursions offered on Thursdays, Saturdays and Sundays

OUTENIQUA CHOO-TJOE

Paul Ash

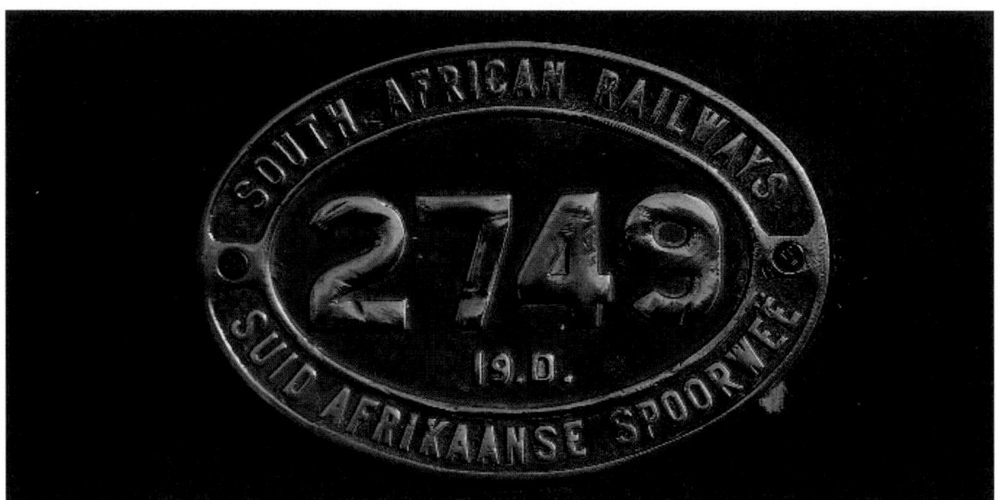

SOMETIMES THE BUREAUCRATS GET IT RIGHT. Whichever South African Railways official came up with the idea to preserve the branch line from George to Knysna on South Africa's fecund Garden Route as the country's official museum railway, then he was a genius. If I ever think of him when I have a glass in my hand, I toast him. The 66km (41-mile) railway was one of the last branch lines to be built in the country. At a time when politicians were falling over themselves to get railways built in all the country districts where there might be votes to be had, it seemed unusual that Knysna, a busy forestry town with a sound shipbuilding industry, should have missed the boom. So I also toast a man named HG Dempster, resident engineer in the coastal town of George who, some time in 1920, was tasked with surveying a route for a proposed railway along the coast to Knysna.

Dempster faced considerable difficulties. This part of the country is called the Garden Route for good reason. Stretching 225km (141 miles) from Mossel Bay in the west to the Storms River mouth in the east, the southern Cape coast is a rugged affair, a narrow coastal plain jammed between the high Outeniqua Mountains to the north and a string of beaches, coves and bays on an otherwise wild and rocky coast. Natural forest grows thickly on the lower flanks of the mountains and in the deep valleys, and fast streams

ABOVE *A bilingual number plate from a THF 19D 4-8-2 No. 2749, one of the rugged workhorses operated by the Outeniqua Choo-Tjoe on the picturesque route between George and Knysna.*

RIGHT *With the Indian Ocean in the background, the much-photographed Kaaimans River bridge on South Africa's Garden Route makes an impressive sight as an eastbound train crosses.*

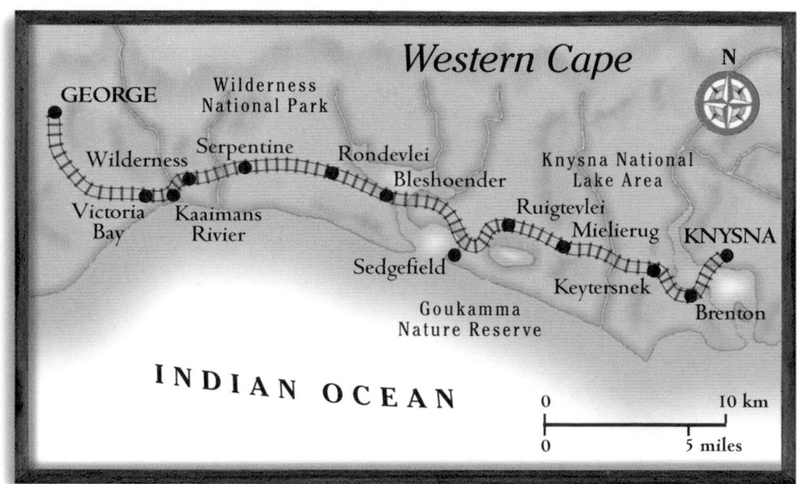

with water the colour of whisky (from tannins in the fynbos vegetation) feed the coastal plain before plunging into the sea.

Engineers usually try to avoid building the kinds of dramatic railways that travellers love. Dempster had little choice. 'The bridgework on this line is exceptionally heavy and if steel bridges had to be provided throughout the total cost would probably be prohibitive', he wrote. There was one thing in his favour, though: the forests that surrounded him were full of hard-wearing yellowwood trees, hundreds of years old and ready for felling. So the first bridges were made of yellowwood. Times have changed, though, and these days a good yellowwood table will cost you thousands of pounds.

George station is a dramatic place to start the journey. The Outeniqua Mountains loom over the town, and if there is an onshore wind the peaks will be shrouded with cloud. The steam locomotive – usually a Class 19D or 24 branch-line engine – eases the train out of the platform at the Outeniqua Transport Museum, at first heading west – the wrong direction – before swinging past the locomotive shed on a 180-degree balloon. My coach is a wooden-bodied, side-door suburban with green leather seats and windows that open all the way. From the right-hand side of the train – the ocean side on eastbound trains – my view was likely to be ocean, beaches, lakes and forest.

George is not a big place, and the train is soon rolling downgrade through open country, pastures spreading out from the track on each side, and then into the extensive pine plantations which generate a considerable chunk of the town's prosperity. I had picked a fine day to ride the train. Although winter, it was sunny, and the smell of pine needles and coal smoke mingled pleasantly in the warm air. Being a low-density branch line, the track is unwelded and I was soon caught up in the rolling gait of the coach bogie – directly under my seat – banging over the gaps between the rails.

LEFT *The morning train from George steams onto the bridge over the lagoon as it heads for Knysna.*

OPPOSITE *Class 24 and 19D steam locomotives slumber at George locomotive depot. The town is home to the Outeniqua Transport Museum, also the departure point for the Outeniqua Choo-Tjoe.*

The pace is quite brisk here as the line drops rapidly down towards the sea. Ten kilometres (6 miles) out of George, the train bursts out of the forest above Victoria Bay, a cluster of old beach houses perched above the sea. The train hugs the cliff face and rattles through a tunnel to emerge high above the Kaaimans River. Crossing the river was Dempster's greatest challenge. In his report he wrote: 'The Kaaimans River presents the most difficult problem in the construction of the line – after considering several alternatives I propose to cross it at the mouth as that appears on the whole to be better than running up the gorge on the west side, crossing it near the junction of the Zwart River and returning to the coast on the east side of the gorge.' Dempster proposed a graceful, 13-arch concrete bridge. A steel superstructure, although cheaper to build, would have been, as he puts it, 'particularly undesirable' for a bridge that actually stands in the breakers at high tide. The result is one of the finest – and most photographed – bridges in Africa, and I had a fine view of it from my window on the right-hand side of the train as we approached. As the train clattered over the bridge, a fisherman standing knee-deep in the shallows beneath one of the arches looked up and waved.

The driver opened the throttle for the short climb up from the bridge, and a plume of white smoke hung in the air to mark our passage. A short whistle for walkers on the beach was sounded as we eased to a stop in Wilderness station. Wilderness marks the beginning of what locals call the Lake District. We were now off the high coastal plain and down at sea level. Although flat, the route was not an easy one for a railway engineer. Between here and Knysna, Dempster's route took the railway past – or over – no fewer than six large vleis (lakes). Where he could, Dempster kept the line on high ground, but a line of rocky, forested hills to the north limited his options. So the railway heads eastward into the lakes, skirting the larger ones and crossing others on low bridges.

Our driver was in no hurry and we drifted along, slowing for the Serpentine, where road and rail share the same bridge. Our progress was gentle enough to leave the grey herons fishing undisturbed in the calm waters of the vleis, and grazing cows and horses could not be bothered to watch us steam by. On one lake, another fisherman waved from his skiff and then turned back to his casting.

At Sedgefield we halted to cross the opposite working from Knysna. The crew cleaned the fire and inspected the locomotive while a Kaapse Klopse (Cape minstrel) band panhandled on the platform. Some passengers wandered into the pie shop in what was once the stationmaster's office. The pies, I can tell you with conviction, are worth travelling a long way to eat.

Soon the rapid beat of an oncoming train could be heard above the minstrels' guitars and banjos, and a trail of white smoke rose above distant pine trees. 'Right time', said our conductor with a smile as he flagged the train into the passing loop. The crews exchanged the single-line tokens and our driver whistled up for departure. The minstrels turned their banjos on the new arrivals, and the pie-makers hauled another batch from the oven.

We made good time to Goukamma, where we paused for the fireman to make a good fire for the climb ahead. A short whistle, and we began to move. As the last coach cleared the station throat, the driver cracked open the regulator and gouts of smoke and steam erupted from the chimney. Cinders and soot rained from the sky. Not a good day to be wearing white, I thought, as the train lurched into the first curve of the hairpin. From here, the railway picks its way around the base of a hill and then bends back on itself in a savage hairpin. A few minutes later, moving at a good lick, we crested the hill above Goukamma.

The driver kept the regulator open all the way to the summit and then shut off for the long downgrade to the Knysna Lagoon. Through the trees I caught a glimpse of an old stone church. 'That's Belvidere', said the guard. 'They buried some English king there.' He was talking about George Rex, the founder and squire of Knysna who, having lost his job as Marshal of the Admiralty when the British gave up the Cape in 1804, came here to seek his fortune. Rex, it was rumoured, was the result of a dalliance between King George III and Hannah Lightfoot. Not quite a king, but something like royalty in these parts.

The train slowed for Knysna. The lagoon presented Dempster with his last task. Although the bridge across the lagoon is not as formidable as the Kaaimans River bridge, it is still an impressive bit of engineering – 123 spans of 5m (15ft) each, resting on pilings. It looks more fragile than it is, I am told. Still, the train moves across it at a gentle pace, wheels clicking over the track joints. A last whistle for the grade crossing at the edge of town, and the train sighed to a halt in Knysna station. 'Aren't you getting off?' asked the guard, seeing me sitting there. No, I said. As interesting as the town is, I had better things to do – like riding the train back through the lakes.

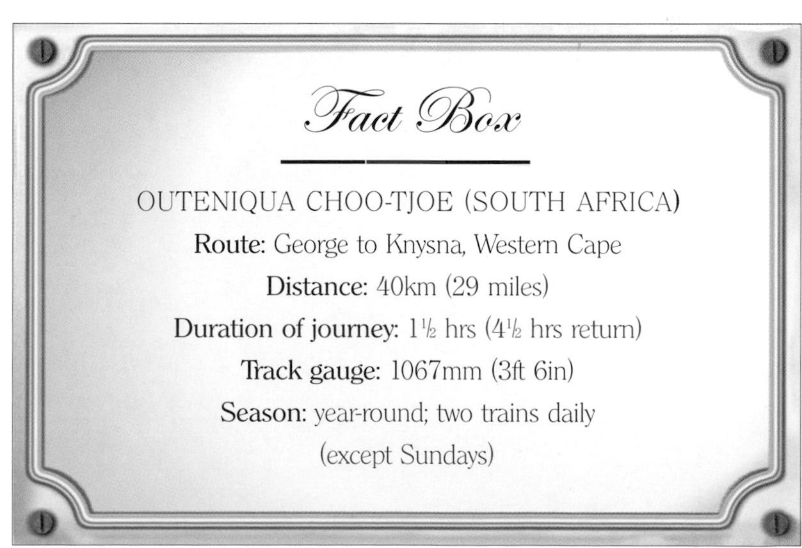

Fact Box

OUTENIQUA CHOO-TJOE (SOUTH AFRICA)

Route: George to Knysna, Western Cape

Distance: 40km (29 miles)

Duration of journey: 1½ hrs (4½ hrs return)

Track gauge: 1067mm (3ft 6in)

Season: year-round; two trains daily (except Sundays)

Asia

Syria & Jordan

THE HEDJAZ RAILWAY

Anthony Lambert

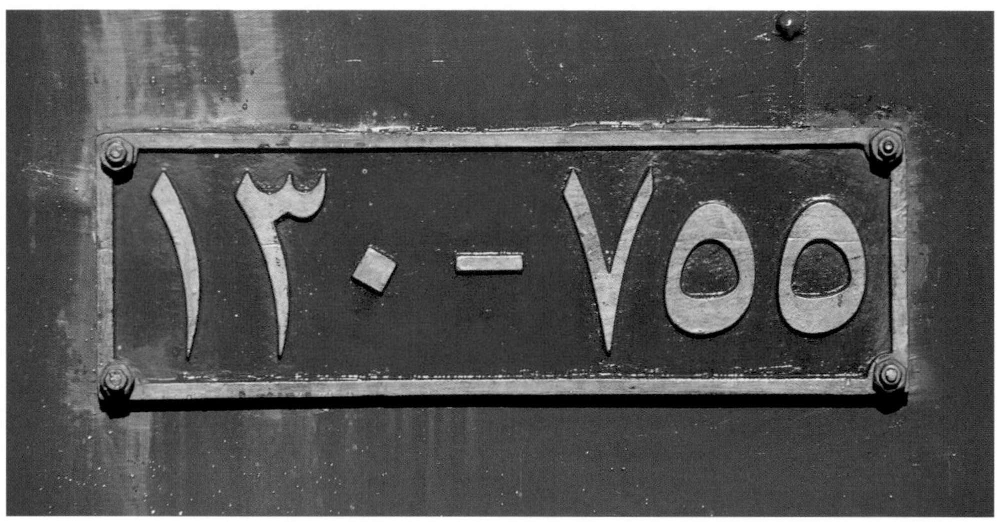

MENTION THE HEDJAZ RAILWAY, and most people are uncertain quite what it was, or is, even though they may have seen David Lean's epic 1962 film *Lawrence of Arabia*. This is hardly surprising, for the film never mentions by name the fascinating railway which TE Lawrence (1888–1935) spent much of his wartime career in the Middle East destroying. Nor have many people used what remains of the passenger services that once carried pilgrims by the hundreds of thousands between Damascus and Medina, Islam's second most holy city and the site of the tomb of the Prophet Mohammed. The only regular service that survives is between the Jordanian capital of Amman and Syria's capital, Damascus, and that runs only twice a week.

ABOVE *The number plate of the Hedjaz Railway's locomotive No. 755, a Swiss-built 2-6-0 tank engine.*

RIGHT *A Jung 2-8-2 No. 51 crosses an impressive double-tier bridge in Jordan's capital, Amman.*

PREVIOUS PAGES *A Nippon 4-6-2 No. 82 tackles the climb out of Amman with a southbound train.*

٥١

The story begins in 1900 when the Ottoman sultan, Abdül Hamid II, announced the building of the Hedjaz Railway (HR) as part of his silver jubilee celebrations. Construction work began in May 1901 from the northern end at Damascus, where the great caravans of pilgrims had traditionally assembled for the annual Haj (pilgrimage to Mecca, birthplace of Mohammed). It took between 30 and 40 arduous days for pilgrims to reach the holy city by foot, camel or donkey; the train would take just two or three days. The intention was to extend the railway beyond Medina to Mecca and even to the port of Jedda on the Red Sea, allowing pilgrims arriving by sea from India to reach Mecca from the south. Because the railway was built primarily for religious purposes (though military and geopolitical considerations were not absent), the plan was to use finance, labour and equipment only from Muslim countries.

Substantial contributions from the Sultan (recognized as the guardian of Islam's holy places) and the Shah of Persia permitted the realization of the first ideal, though most of the money came from poor people and even schoolchildren. It was said that the HR was the only project carried out by the Ottoman empire in which money was not siphoned off by venal officials. However, the second two ideals had to be quickly abandoned when it became apparent that the Islamic world could supply neither the skills nor the materials. The man placed in charge of construction was well chosen: Oberingenieur Heinrich Meissner had already built railways within the Ottoman empire and was fluent in Turkish, English and Italian, as well as his native German. But even Meissner Pasha, as he was honoured, was allowed only as far south as El Ula, 338km (211 miles) north of Medina, and had to rely on his Muslim assistant to be his eyes and ears.

With major input from the Ottoman army, which provided skilled labour and protected the works from Arab tribesmen, who were none too keen on the railway, Meissner built the 1320km (825 miles) between the original terminus in Damascus, at Cadem, and Medina within seven years. The official opening took place in September 1908, though sections had been opened to traffic as they were completed. The railway was built to the curious gauge of 1050mm (3ft 5¼in), which derived from an earlier concession granted to a French company to build a railway over the Lebanon and Anti-Lebanon mountains between Beirut and Damascus; this specified a gauge of between 1.05 and 1.45m (3½–4¾ft), and the company chose the minimum figure. It obviously made sense to build the Hedjaz Railway to the same gauge.

ABOVE *A Swiss-built 2-6-0T stands in front of Damascus Kanawat station. The station was opened in 1911 when the northern terminus of the Hedjaz Railway was extended from the original terminus at Cadem.*

It was never expected that the HR would have an easy life. The harsh climate of the Arabian interior made water supplies for both locomotives and staff at the intermediate stations and crossing points a major problem. Tanks, cisterns and wells were built, but water trains were a continual feature of the HR. When rain did fall, it tended to come in quantities large enough to cause flash floods over the rocky ground, compelling Meissner to build much of the railway on an embankment and to create sufficient culverts and even viaducts over wadis (dry riverbeds) to withstand and dissipate the flood waters. This amounted to 1960 culverts and bridges over the length of the line.

The anticipated hostility of the Arabs to the railway was reflected in the design of the station buildings, which were built to be defensible, with firing slits in the perimeter walls. Resentment toward the railway, as with the telegraph before it, was based on a fear that it would assist the Ottoman Turks in strengthening their hold over Arabia. Local Bedouin tribesmen had also made a practice of exacting 'tolls' from pilgrims making the Haj; this source of income would be destroyed by the railway. The severity of disruption caused by tribal assaults during construction varies according to the source, but it was not long after the opening of the section through to Medina that serious trouble arose with the arrest of tribal leaders. Bedouin raids escalated into an attack on Medina while much of the garrison was away working on the railway, and the remnants only just held out until reinforcements arrived. The severity of tribal opposition to the railway as far as Medina effectively ruled out the planned extension to Mecca and Jedda, and only a small amount of work was carried out south of Medina.

When World War I broke out in 1914, Col. TE Lawrence found fertile soil when, in 1916, he was appointed adviser to Prince Faisal (1885–1933), the leader of the Arab revolt against the Turks; the idea of blowing up bridges and looting trains on the hated railway appealed enormously to the irregular forces that Lawrence mustered. It was impossible for the Turks to secure the entire length of the railway, so it was easy to find remote sections for an ambush, although the more lightly garrisoned stations were also attacked and destroyed. The tactic was to impede rather than stop railway movements. Closing the railway would have freed up Turkish troops to fight elsewhere, and Lawrence's forces relied on the passage of supply trains to expropriate small arms and ammunition.

ABOVE *A Nippon 4-6-2 No. 82, with a water tank behind the tender, in the desert south of Amman. Hundreds of bridges had to be built along the route of the HR to withstand occasional flash flooding.*

During one of many hit-and-run raids, Lawrence took away a station bell, which he brought back to England and had in his rooms at All Souls College in Oxford; the poet Robert Graves, in his memoir, *Goodbye to All That*, says that the bell came from Tell Shawm, but the definitive history of the railway – *Hedjaz Railway* by R Tourret – gives Shatum. The combination of Lawrence's exploits and occasional bombing raids on major installations such as locomotive depots wrought such damage to the railway that the southern 862km (539 miles) beyond Ma'an to Medina were never fully reopened. However, some trains did run: in 1924, it was noted that a train of returning pilgrims took 12 days to travel between Medina and Ma'an. But heavy rains that year did such damage that the railway was finally closed south of Ma'an, and the trains derailed by Lawrence's forces slowly rusted away, stripped by tribesmen of anything of use.

In the early 1960s it looked as though resurrection was at hand: in 1963 a British company was contracted to rehabilitate the line south of Ma'an, and new bridges were constructed. Tracklaying had crossed the border into Saudi Arabia, but in the early 1970s enthusiasm for the HR's revival waned and work was abandoned. Although the railway to Medina has never reopened, the section between El Hasa and Batn et Ghul was incorporated into the Aqaba Railway, which has conveyed phosphates from mines at El Hassa to the sea since 1975.

By the early 1970s there were no longer passenger trains on the Jordanian section of the Hedjaz Railway, but in 1979 protracted negotiations finally bore fruit and a tour was run from Britain to travel by steam over various sections of the HR. From Amman special trains have operated over the Hedjaz Jordan Railway (HJR) south to Qatrana and north to Mafraq, while from Damascus Chemins de Fer Syriens (Syrian Railways) has operated trains between Damascus and Dera'a for the branch line to Bosra. An alternative and regular way to experience the journey between the two capitals is the twice-weekly international diesel-hauled mixed train, which takes nine hours to cover the 223km (139 miles), with a locomotive change at Dera'a.

The HR has always had a very heterogeneous collection of locomotives, from varied sources, and this still applies to the few survivors. Among the locomotives that have been steamed for the benefit of visitors to the HJR over the years are 2-6-2 tank No. 61 (built by Haine St. Pierre in 1955), Nippon Sharyo Pacific No. 82 of 1953, Jung 2-8-2 No. 51 of 1955, 2-8-2 No. 71 (Haine St. Pierre, 1955) and 2-8-2 No. 23 (Robert Stephenson Hawthorn, 1952). In Syria, the locomotives used over the HR are German-built 2-8-0s and 2-8-2s. Locomotives on the HR had a tough life. Quite apart from the sandstorms that cause havoc with moving parts, the original determination to use Muslim engine drivers, who were drawn mostly from the Turkish navy, had unhappy consequences. As one historian of the railway has put it, 'the fatalistic ideas [of Muslims] were unsuited to such a profession' and as early as 1907 the locomotive works yards were full of engines awaiting repair after only four or five months' service, thanks to ignorance or neglect.

RIGHT *A Jung 2-8-2 No. 53 hauls a passenger service north of Amman. The gradients on the southward climb out of Amman were sufficiently steep to warrant the use of Mallets, mostly 2-4-6-0 tender locomotives but also some 0-6-6-0 tanks.*

6025
٥٣

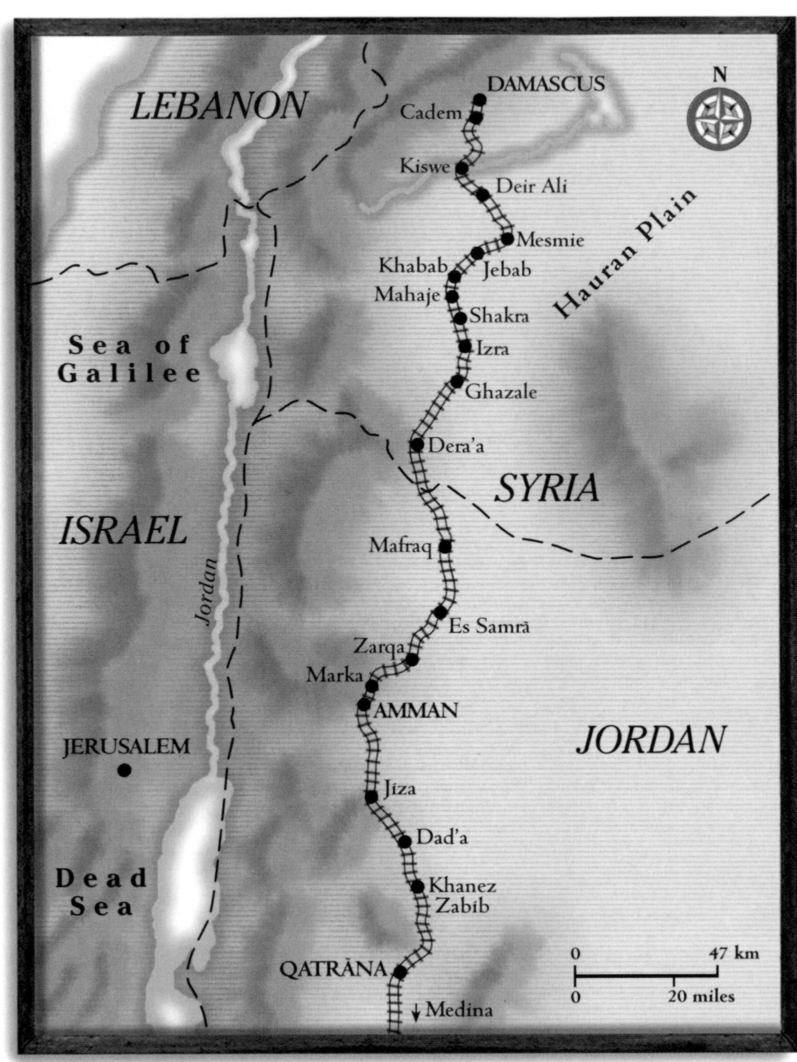

The northern terminus of the HR is the splendidly ornate stone station at Damascus Kanawat, designed by a German architect named Palmer and opened on 31 December 1911 as an extension from the original terminus, 3km (2 miles) away at Cadem. The double-storey booking hall gives on to open platforms which serve other routes as well as the HR line to Amman. Once the ubiquitous pall of pollution hanging over the capital has been left behind, the scenery on the Syrian section is as featureless as the gently undulating gradient profile would suggest. In Syria, all the best railway landscapes are to be found on what remains of the east–west lines to the Mediterranean coast; from the windows of HR trains the constant view is of the parched rock and sand of the Hauran Plain, occasionally interrupted by irrigated crops.

Dera'a was the junction for a branch of the HR running from Haifa, which was chosen in preference to Beirut as the port through which railway materials would be imported. Until its closure in 1949, the railway linking Haifa and Dera'a had the distinction of having the lowest point below sea level of any railway in the world: Jisr el Majame, where the railway crossed the River Jordan, is 246.5m (808½ft) below sea level. Dera'a is also junction for the branch to Bosra, which terminates beside extensive Roman remains.

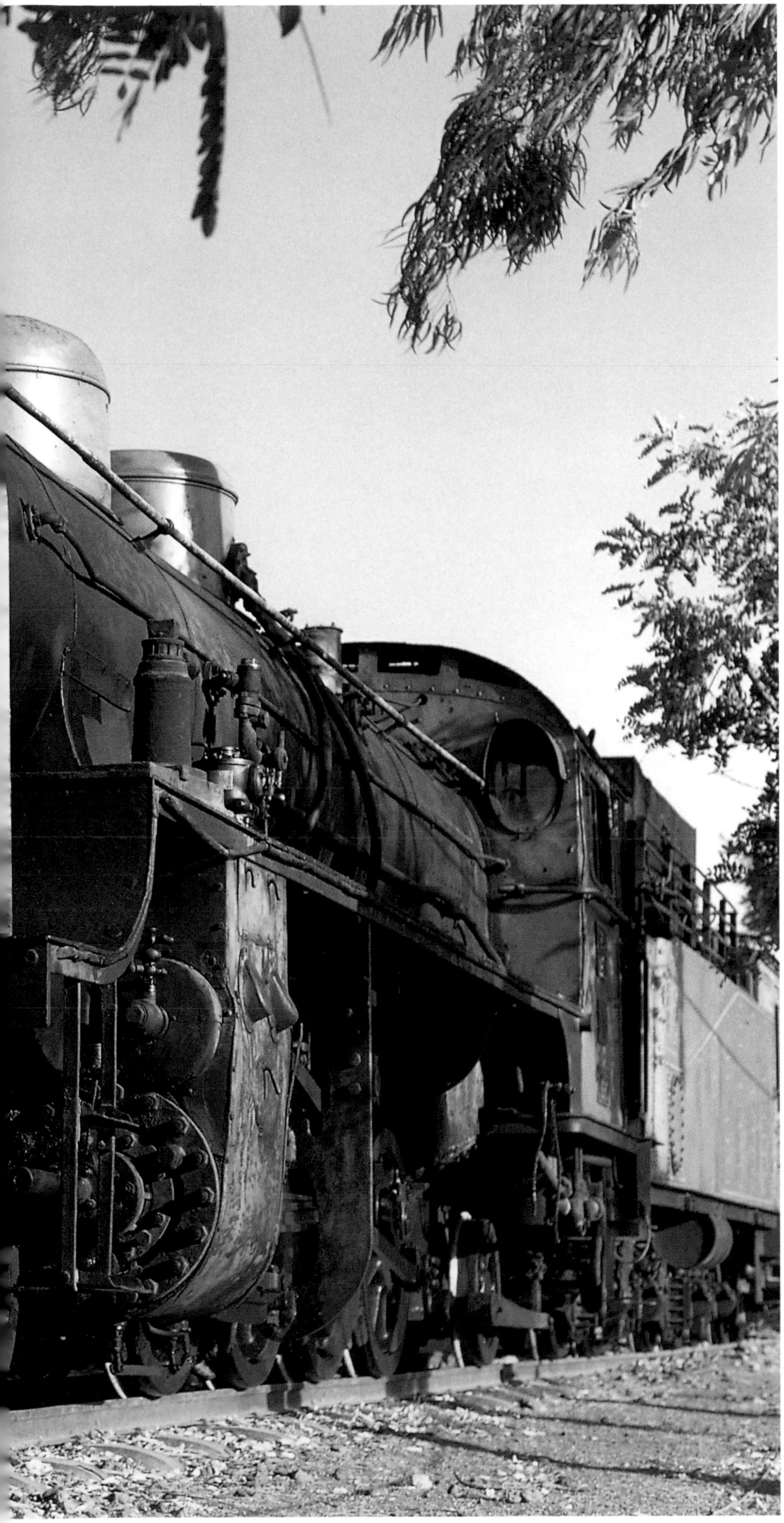

South of Dera'a and over the border into Jordan, the railway has to climb 209m (685ft) through low hills but crossing several examples of Meissner's superb masonry work as the railway crosses broad wadis. The railway facilities in Jordan's capital bear witness to the fact that Amman was an unimportant village when the railway was built, its growth since World War II being exceptional. Here is no multi-platformed station spanned by an imposing overall roof, but a modest station building and locomotive shed more befitting a country junction than a city of over 1.3 million people.

South of the city on the journey to the limit of passenger operations at Qatrana, the landscape is much more interesting than the northern section of the HR. The climb out of Amman on to a plateau is spectacular, the line having to weave round the hills on tight bends to lift it 941m (3087ft) in just 12km (7½ miles). This section also includes the largest civil engineering structure on the entire route, a 60m-high (196ft) 10-arched viaduct with lower relieving arches. White concrete houses and flats cover the hills as the train barks through the suburbs and a short tunnel and into open country.

At first the bleached sand and scrub grasses are interspersed with flashes of green where irrigated crops are growing, some in polytunnels. But soon all sign of human activity, apart from the two lines of steel, is left behind. The only intrusions are the periodic stations or crossing points, the solid, stone two-storey buildings standing gaunt and often roofless beside the line, or the remains of the blockhouses or forts built to house a protecting garrison. It is here, in a landscape with nothing but tufts of hardy grass baking under the unremitting sun, that you wonder at the achievement of Meissner and his men in building this railway. They laboured in extreme heat, slept in often freezing temperatures, were subject to attack from tribesmen and liable to cholera, dysentery, typhoid or scurvy. Every morsel of food and almost every drop of water to sustain the thousands of men had to be brought into this inhospitable terrain, which extended all the way to Medina. No wonder they made Meissner a pasha.

LEFT *This Hartmann 2-8-2 No. 260 of 1918, was one of a batch of locomotives supplied to the Hedjaz Railway at the end of World War I.*

Fact Box

HEDJAZ RAILWAY (SYRIA & JORDAN)

Route: Damascus to Amman, or Qatrana

Distance: 329km (206 miles)

Duration of journey: 9 hours (Damascus–Amman)

Track gauge: 1050mm (3ft 5¼in)

Season: twice weekly

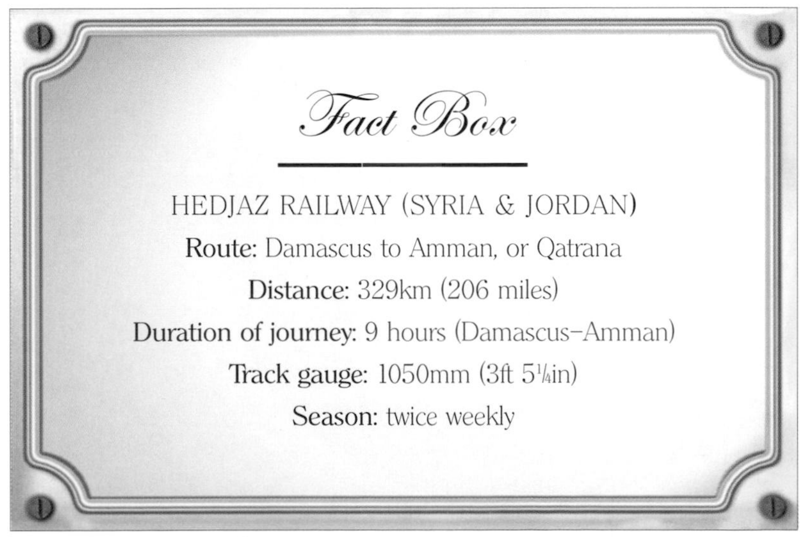

Pakistan

CHANGA MANGA FOREST RAILWAY

Peter Lemmey

IT'S THAT MISTY TIME JUST BEFORE DAWN BREAKS. Somewhere nearby a rooster is awake. Across the Forest Officer's compound, individual trees and small buildings emerge from the shadows of a Punjab night. Shrouded figures move between three small steam engines, tending the fires as steam-raising gets under way. Plumes of pale smoke rise in the cool morning air. Today is a public holiday in Pakistan, and in an hour or so's time, when the sun has risen above the trees, the first visitors will arrive here at Changa Manga ready for a ride out into the forest behind one of these narrow gauge locomotives. The 600mm (2ft) gauge system at Changa Manga is a remarkable survivor among steam railways, having quietly evolved in recent years from an obscure logging line into a unique piece of Pakistan's railway heritage.

Changa Manga forest covers some 4860ha (12,000 acres) of the Punjab about 100km (62½ miles) south of Lahore and not far from the Indian border. Although the Himalayan foothills are barely 200km (125 miles) to the north, this is flat, lowland country. The forest at Changa Manga is man-made and is claimed to be the first of its kind in the world. It lies east of the small town of the same name on the broad gauge main line running southward from Lahore to Karachi.

ABOVE *The brass plate on the Andrew Barclay engine bears the name of Parry, the famous machinery importers founded in the 18th century.*

RIGHT *Early morning at Change Manga during the Eid holiday at the end of Ramadan, with all three engines raising steam and a busy day in prospect.*

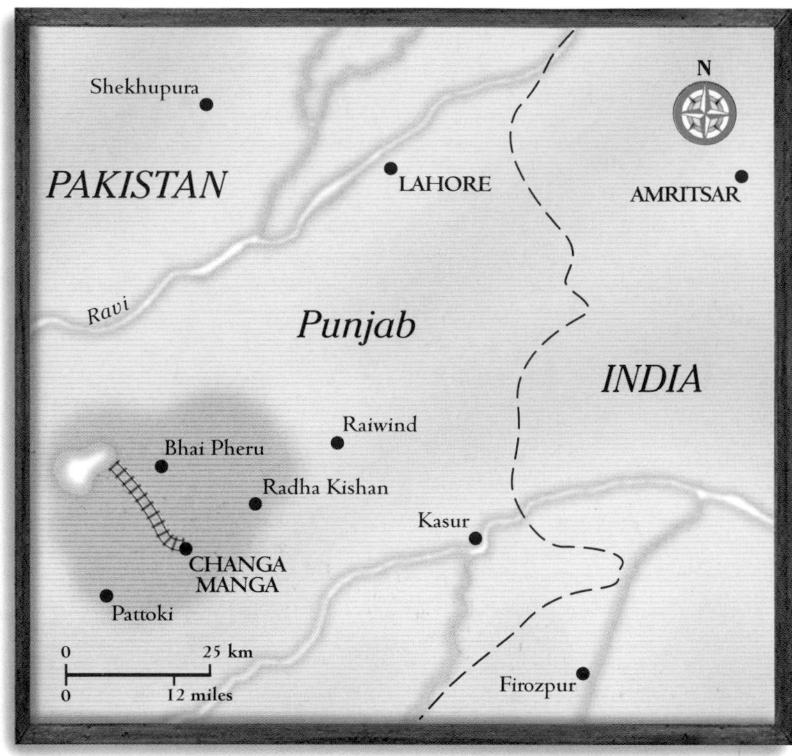

As the sun rises, the layout of this forestry depot becomes evident. Narrow gauge railway track spreads out in all directions, with extensive sidings and yards serving areas set aside for seasoning timber. Here and there, sections of track and spare wagons are stacked up as though on a giant model railway, ready for use on temporary lines extending out in the forest. At the engine shed beneath the trees the three locomotives – two 0-6-0s and a 0-4-0 – are being watered and loaded with a mixture of coal and wood for the day ahead.

As long ago as 1865, it was the coming of main-line railways to this part of what was then British India that led to plans to establish a forest here. In those days the Punjab Railway was being extended southward from Lahore. Its early locomotives were wood-burners and the company needed to secure its own source of fuel. With the extension of the rail network to the Indian coalfields in the east the railways turned to coal firing, but even so their demand for timber products went on growing, and by the early 20th century 200ha (500 acres) of forest were being harvested annually at Changa Manga, with the help of the narrow gauge railway. By this time the old Punjab line had been absorbed by the great North Western Railway of India, which served the vast territory between Delhi and the Khyber Pass up until independence and the creation of the Pakistan/India border in 1947.

These little locomotives at Changa Manga, running up and down the yard in the morning sun ready to work trains of holiday visitors up to the lake in the woods, are the legacy of a time when steam engines worked scores of industrial and forestry lines across the subcontinent. Whether hauling cane to sugar mills or moving soil at

RIGHT *A timeless narrow gauge scene on the Changa Manga line, as the crew of the Andrew Barclay locomotive take the author on a tour of the railway.*

irrigation projects, industrial steam power working on the narrow gauge was the prescription wherever heavy loads needed to be worked economically over short distances. Extracting timber from Changa Manga and bringing it down for seasoning and treating before sending it away on the main line was a task suited to a 600mm (2ft) gauge railway, and the line still operates timber trains when required.

The engineers of British India sent their orders for new engines back to the home country. The city of Leeds, in Yorkshire, was once a prolific source of small locomotives, from a variety of builders: the two 0-6-0s at Changa Manga were built by the firm of John Fowler & Co Ltd., one in 1927 and the other in 1936. The even smaller 0-4-0 hails, however, from Scotland, a product of Andrew Barclay Sons & Co. Ltd. of Kilmarnock. That these engines, built for immediate hard work in faraway places, are still running today is a tribute to their original makers and to local ingenuity.

The main road from Lahore crosses the railway between the yard and the passenger station, barely more than a low platform beside the road. On this holiday morning, buses and cars are already arriving, bringing families with children and their cool-boxes and Thermos flasks. One or two of the more inquisitive arrivals wander down the yard to where the two Fowler locomotives are marshalling trains of home-made coaches. Before this pair can pull forward up to the road crossing and pick up their first payloads of the day, the Barclay 0-4-0 emerges from the carriage shed with a string of cream-painted saloon coaches even smaller than the others. Several have armchairs inside and at least one has an air-conditioning unit. This little train heads away over the road crossing, but rather than stopping for passsengers it sets off down a branch line which follows the main road, eventually disappearing among the trees.

The holiday train service from the station by the road up through the stands of timber to Mehtabi Lake takes about half an hour. Members of the Forest Officer's staff issue paper tickets. Many of the family groups have come smartly dressed and one gets a strong impression of well-heeled city families on a day out: more than a trace of expensive scent hangs in the air, mingling with the engine smoke.

The railway runs through woodland interspersed with open tracts of ground where trees have recently been felled; the forest is more a managed plantation than wild jungle. The trees themselves are chiefly mulberry and shishan, and shelter plenty of wildlife. Kingfishers can be seen where the line crosses the many drainage channels; deer are visible among the trees, and Changa Manga is also known for its vulture colonies. As the 0-6-0 and its train steam east towards the lake a number of branch lines peel off to serve other parts of the forest. A last burst of speed brings the train up over an irrigation bridge and into the lakeside station; as the engine turns on a triangle ready to return for another load of visitors, the passengers stroll off round the lake: the tea stall seems a popular first stop.

Many years ago the North Western Railway's forestry department built within the forest a guesthouse for visiting officials. It is a spacious gabled building, its garden shaded by fir trees, the white gates at the bottom of the drive presided over by a couple of watchmen. Located a mile or so from the Forest Officer's compound, the guesthouse is served by a long, looping branch of the forest railway network, though one that is seemingly not often used. However, at holiday weekends families from Lahore come and stay at the lodge for a day or two away from the city. These guests have a train at their disposal for picnic trips into the forest – and this is where we saw the 0-4-0 and its coaches hurrying off to in the early morning, ready to take up their position at the end of the guesthouse drive.

The run to Mehtabi Lake covers only one section of the rail network here. There are about 25km (16 miles) of permanent track within the forest, and it is quite feasible to make a more comprehensive tour of the system if one turns up during the week. One engine is usually in steam whether or not there is any logging going on, and it is therefore possible for visitors to rent a train of their own by the hour. This is a rare treat: there must be few, if any, other places where you can hire your own steam train with such minimal delay – and for such minimal outlay.

The welcome from the staff, even to strangers arriving from another continent unannounced, is as warm as you come to expect in this most friendly of countries: 'Pakistan peoples are A1 for friendly', as one railwayman quaintly but accurately puts it. It doesn't take long for them to make up a train and all is soon ready for the start of what should be a highly enjoyable journey. With your own train, you can explore further into the forest and stop to take photographs, have a picnic or just take in the scene. With only the hiss of steam from the engine and the bird-calls in the trees to break the silence, it makes a railway idyll difficult to improve on.

ABOVE *A John Fowler engine built in 1927 brings in a train of timber destined for the Changa Manga sawmill. The forest was orignally established to provide wood for locomotives on the old Punjab Railway.*

OPPOSITE *The Changa Manga railway crosses numerous irrigation channels. These carry meltwater from Kashmir into the mighty Indus River.*

Fact Box

CHANGA MANGA FOREST RAILWAY (PAKISTAN)

Route: Changa Manga Forest circuit (from main line junction to Mehtabi Lake), Punjab province

Distance: Up to 25km (16 miles)

Duration of journey: 2 hrs to full day

Gauge: 600mm (2ft)

Season: morning departures on Fridays and public holidays; at other times by arrangement

Australia

THE GREAT ZIG ZAG RAILWAY

Susan Storm

A PLUME OF SOOTY SMOKE RISES THROUGH THE TALL EUCALYPTUS TREES of the Blue Mountains, 130km (80 miles) west of Sydney. The piercing whistle of a steam train cuts through the tough Australian terrain to send flocks of squawking sulphur-crested cockatoos airborne. The mountains, which are named for the hazy blue light refracting off the oily eucalyptus leaves, resemble a grey, velvety blanket flung over a landscape that had long been a formidable natural barrier between Sydney and the arable land to the west. The Blue Mountains form part of the Great Dividing Range, a rocky, impenetrable region, peaking at more than 1000m (3280ft) above sea level, and stretching from Victoria's Gippsland in the south to Queensland's tropical rainforests in the north.

I've come to ride the historic Zig Zag Railway, which has been acclaimed as one of the greatest engineering achievements of the Victorian age. It was built between 1866 and 1869, as part of the Great Western Main Railway from Sydney to Bathurst, to develop the coal, steel and iron-ore industries in the Lithgow Valley, to export oil refined from shale deposits in the area, and to move produce and people from the rich agricultural regions west of the Blue Mountains to Sydney.

ABOVE *Volunteer driver Larry Zanker polishes the controls on the footplate of the Zig Zag Railway's historic locomotive No. 1072,* City of Lithgow.

RIGHT *A view of No. 2 Viaduct, with No 3. Viaduct visible at left, illustrates the scale of the achievement of the Zig Zag's Victorian builders.*

PREVIOUS PAGES *Hauled by the* City of Lithgow, *a train steams over the five stone arches of No. 1 Viaduct on the Zig Zag Railway.*

ABOVE *On days when steam services are not running, the Zig Zag Railway carries visitors in vintage Queensland Railways diesel railcars.*

I step across the sandy tracks that disappear into the bush, and onto tiny Clarence station, which nestles against a bristly, dry copse of trees. Immediately I enter another time: although I can imagine the wide skirts and portmanteaus of early travellers, there is no romance on this line. The trains that worked here represented the blood, sweat and tears of the pioneers. Now, though, the train is run by volunteers, whose objective is to keep a piece of Australian railway history alive.

Inside the cream-and-red-painted wooden station, the ticket seller is in no hurry, for the wooden arms of the painted clock are fixed at 11:00, and the train is only going down the hill and back again. The platform is abuzz with excited children and visitors of all nations and cultures, most of whom have never seen a steam engine. It's taken me two and a half hours to get here from Sydney – longer than the 1½-hour, 8km (5-mile) train ride I'm about to do.

When the Great Western Main Railway from Sydney reached Clarence, the highest railway station in the Blue Mountains (1115m/3658ft above sea level), the engineers then had to find a way to descend the 209m (687ft) down the Lithgow Valley. The choice was to cut a 3.2km-long (2-mile) tunnel, which would have required some 10 million bricks, or to build a zigzag railway – the easiest and most economical method with the technology and materials available. The enterprising and often ruthless John Whitton, chief engineer of the New South Wales Government Railways, undertook the prodigious feat of building a railway line through the seemingly impenetrable terrain that separated the valleys.

The Lithgow Zig Zag finally opened in 1869. The line is a series of gently sloping ramps forming the letter Z, connected at the extremities by reversing stations known as Top Points and Bottom Points. Two long tunnels and three impressive sandstone viaducts – all hand-cut – mark the passage as it winds along narrow man-made ledges that cling to the mountainside.

The Zig Zag Railway today operates trains on the Top and Middle Bars of the 'Great Lithgow Zig Zag', between Clarence and Bottom Points. There are three stops on the route: on Top Road at No. 1 Viaduct, for the best view of the Zig Zag; at Top Points to see the site of the 1901 runaway and reverse direction; and at Bottom Points, for a tour through the workshops, where the locomotives and rolling stock are maintained and repaired.

Life during construction was tough. The men lived in tents, often working in near-freezing temperatures. Surveyors were winched down the cliffs in wicker baskets to shoot the surveying line in, and rubble had to be removed by wheel-barrow or else thrown down the mountainside into the surrounding forest. The demands of the Zig Zag route necessitated the development of locomotive boilers able to cope with steep gradients, and the lessons learned here were helpful for the building of other mountain railways.

Whitton commanded his crew from a seat in a carved rock ledge, using runners or horsemen, semaphore or mirrors to convey his instructions. He won the bitter arguments over the advantages of steel rails over iron, as well as the durability of iron bridges over wooden ones. The hand-carved viaducts, culverts and bridges have endured because of Whitton's determination to use the hard local stone, transported by horse-drawn cart from the quarry 1km (⅔ mile) away. The Italian stonemasons who worked on the line used metric measuring equipment rather than imperial, marking the first use of the metric system in Australia.

The Zig Zag was originally planned to have five sandstone viaducts and three tunnels, but only three viaducts and two tunnels were built. The third tunnel developed cracks during construction and had to be blown up to form a cutting. In the late 19th century, when the original Zig Zag could no longer cope with the volume of rail traffic, a 10-tunnel deviation was constructed through the escarpment. The deviation, which opened in 1910, begins 5km (3 miles) east of Clarence.

Soon after the deviation opened, the Zig Zag became obsolete. The track was removed and the site reclaimed by the bush. But in 1972, a group of young railway enthusiasts, keen to establish a tourist steam railway in New South Wales, formed a non-profit co-operative. They rebuilt the line and began purchasing old rolling stock to restore. Track was re-laid on the 1.5km (1-mile) Middle Road, and in 1975 limited train operations began for tourists and train enthusiasts. The gauge was changed from the New South Wales standard of 1478mm (4ft 8½in) to 1097mm (3ft 6in) when the co-op could no longer buy rolling stock from the NSW Railways (because they were establishing a museum of their own). Most of the stock was obtained from Queensland, and the rest from South Australia, Western Australia and Tasmania.

Larry Zanker, co-driver for the day and an industrial chemist in his day job, bends over the wheels in a cloud of gritty steam. 'I've been doing this for 25 years', he yells, adjusting his checked cap with its driver's brass badge. 'It took ten years to learn to drive this train, that's hundreds of hours. It keeps me off the streets.'

Colin Kay, one-armed volunteer train guard, blows his whistle and waves the green flag. 'All aboard!' he shouts, and the train rolls off into the valley. In the 19th century, when there was only one brake on the train and one on the engine, it took three hours to negotiate the Zig Zag. Today it takes a minimum of one and a half hours.

On the footplate with Geoff Moran, a tax officer by day, Zanker throws a shovelful of coal into the blazing, hungry furnace. We're almost knocked back by the heat, which reaches 2000 degrees. The train is hauled by locomotive No. 1072, *City of Lithgow*, a 4-6-2 (Pacific) express passenger engine built in 1956 at Walkers Ltd., in Maryborough, Queensland. The *City of Lithgow* was first based in Brisbane and later at Toowoomba, Queensland, until it was taken out of service in 1970. The engine is also known as the 'Bety' after its telegraphic code. It was bought by the Zig Zag in 1975 and named in grateful recognition of the support of the people of Lithgow.

The train rushes into the 493m-long (1617ft) Clarence Tunnel, the highest railway tunnel in Australia. We steam out into the light, through copses of eucalypts towards Mt. Sinai Halt, along Top Road, which runs parallel to the main road, then past Edgecombe Siding towards No. 1 Viaduct. It's the first of the three viaducts along the route, with a magnificent seven-arch span on a 10-chain curve. The train stops so that passengers can view the railway's three levels: Top Road, with No. 1 viaduct in front; Middle Road, with viaducts 2 and 3; and the double electric line of the original Bottom Road, which still carries the main line to distant Perth, Western Australia.

At Top Points Lookout, the *City of Lithgow* is uncoupled and shunted to the front for a fill-up of water before pulling out. From Top Points the train crosses No. 2 Viaduct, then No. 3 Viaduct and continues to Cockerton Place Halt, a popular picnic and barbeque area, right below No. 1 Viaduct. It continues through Middle Road Tunnel No. 2, and past the locomotive depot on the way to Bottom Points station, where passengers can alight and tour the workshops for closer views of maintenance work and the restoration of rolling stock owned by the co-operative.

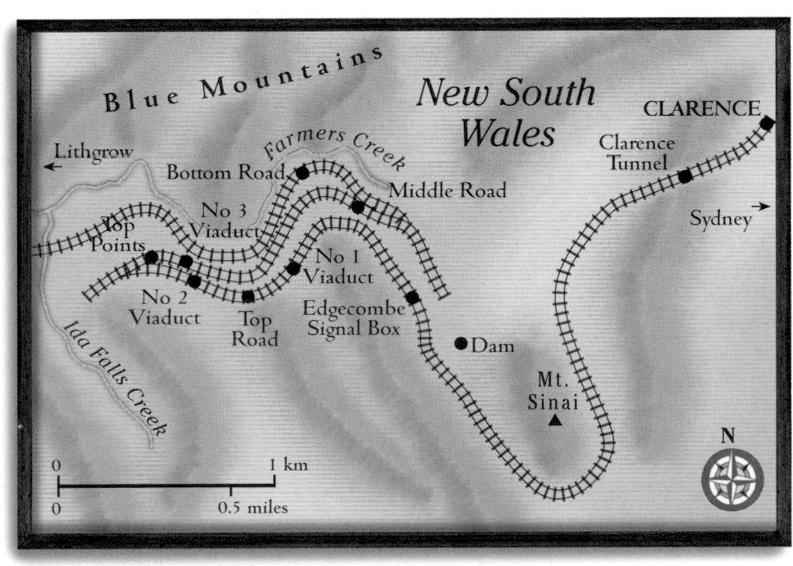

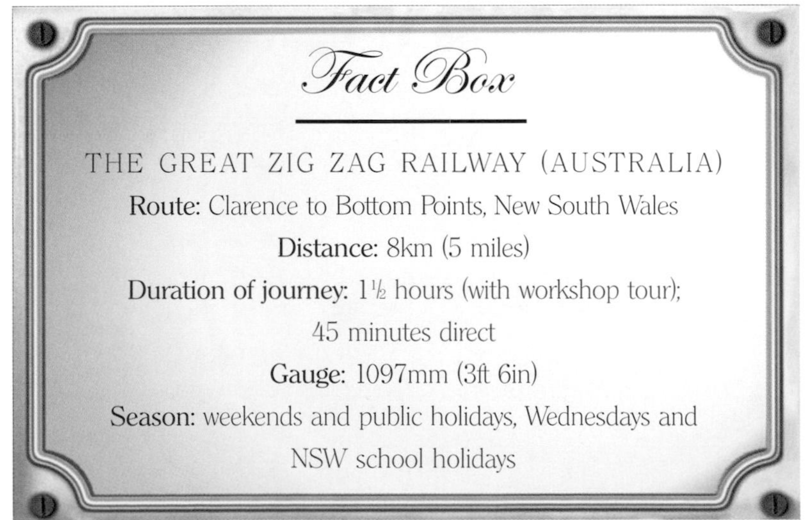

THE PICHI RICHI RAILWAY

Philip Game

IT IS 10:30AM ON A BRIGHT SPRING SUNDAY MORNING in the sleepy South Australian Outback town of Quorn, population 1400. If the wide, sun-scorched streets are not exactly bustling, there is a palpable sense of anticipation as families, seniors and railway enthusiasts converge on the town's stucco-fronted station, which faces a row of four two-storeyed hotels with overhanging verandahs – quintessential Aussie pubs.

Quorn's unspoilt streetscapes have formed the backdrop for several Australian movies, including *Sunday Too Far Away* (1974) and *Gallipoli* (1981). The town is located 340km (211 miles) north of Adelaide – around four hours' drive – and 41km (25 miles) northeast of Port Augusta. Quorn lies in the lower reaches of the Flinders Ranges, a landscape which inspired both the Aboriginal rock painters thousands of years ago and their more recent successors, such as landscape painter Sir Hans Heysen (1877–1968). Silhouetted against vast skies, the purple-hued mountains – eroded stumps of an ancient mountain system – rise majestically above the grey saltbush plains. Looping around the immense crater-like bowl of Wilpena Pound, the ridgelines march off towards the desolate salt lakes of the interior. Disdainful emus stalk the plains, and kangaroos and rock wallabies materialize around dusk. The many evocative stone ruins recall the hardship and heartbreak of pioneer European settlement in this harsh environment.

This dramatic landscape is the setting for the Pichi Richi Railway, which preserves the last remaining operating section of The Ghan, the historic Central Australian Railway. Formed in 1973, the Pichi Richi Railway Preservation Society runs the railway as a working museum, operating steam trains between Quorn, Woolshed Flat and the city of Port Augusta at least once a week from Easter through October. Operated entirely by unpaid enthusiasts, the Pichi Richi is distinguished by its striking scenery, stone embankments

ABOVE *The insignia of the Pichi Richi Railway evokes the rugged grandeur of South Australia's Flinders Ranges.*

RIGHT *The Pichi Richi Railway's steam locomotive No. 933 leaves Quorn with the Pichi Richi Explorer, bound for Port Augusta.*

WANDANA
W
933

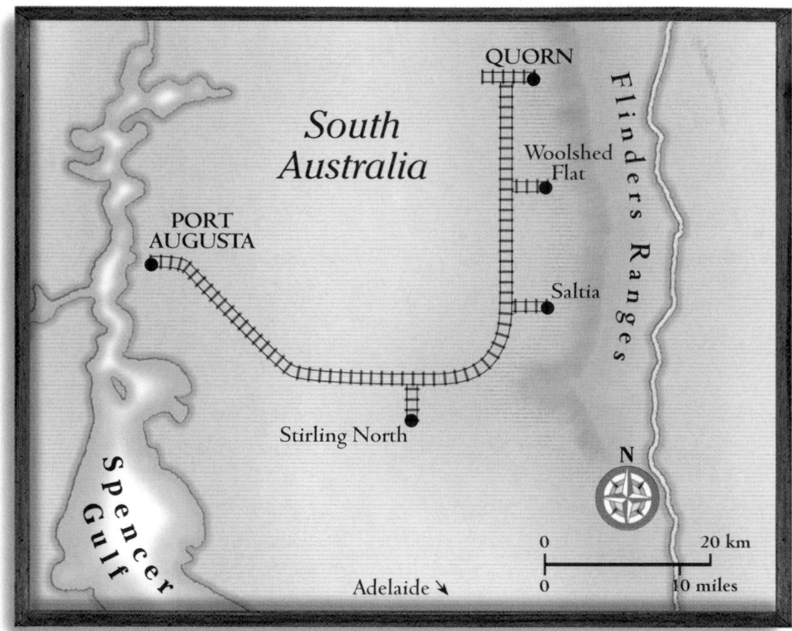

LEFT *Quorn station, headquarters of the Pichi Richi Railway. In the first half of the 20th century, the town was an important rail junction.*

OPPOSITE *The Pichi Richi's W Class 4-8-2 No. 933 shunts at Woolshed Flat, the halfway point between Quorn and Port Augusta.*

and iron bridges. Carriages are usually antique, timber-bodied stock from the old South Australian Railways and the Commonwealth Railways. In July 2004 the society celebrated 30 years of operations.

The railway was born out of the vain hopes of 19th-century European pioneers that 'rain would follow the plough'. Their efforts were buoyed by a few good years before the arid climate of South Australia reasserted itself. Wheat farming inevitably failed, but copper mining and sheep and cattle grazing stimulated the survey of a railway running northward from Port Augusta on Spencer Gulf, crossing the Pichi Richi Pass and following the Flinders Ranges north to present-day Marree.

The Pichi Richi Railway opened in 1879, the first stage of a Great Northern Railway. In 1929 this line reached Alice Springs, but an extension to Darwin took another 74 years, a landmark celebrated on 15 January 2004 when the first freight train to cross Australia from north to south was met in Stirling North by a PRR double-headed special, the two trains running parallel into Port Augusta!

The east–west railway traversing the Nullarbor Plain was completed in 1917, and for the next 20 years travellers crossing the continent went via the Pichi Richi Pass. For years, five changes of train were required to cross Australia, thanks to the differing track gauges laid down in the 19th century. As a result, Quorn became a vital railway junction, and the town grew with the railways. However, repeated flood damage and the limitations of the existing route necessitated the construction of a standard gauge track from Stirling North (just outside Port Augusta) to Brachina, west of the Flinders Ranges, and the narrow gauge PRR was closed to regular traffic in 1957.

After the standard gauge line from Port Augusta to Marree was opened in 1956, the 1067mm (3ft 6in) narrow gauge track that ran northward from Hawker was progressively closed and removed. Eventually the dual gauge track spanning the 7km (4 miles) from the terminus at Stirling North to Port Augusta was torn up. In 2000, the Pichi Richi Railway Preservation Society (PRRPS) began restoring this line, which crosses the causeway over Spencer Gulf. An inaugural steam train ran from Quorn to Port Augusta on 29 March 2003. In February 2004, the Pichi Richi Railway celebrated jointly with the Great Southern Railway, the private-sector operator of the 'new' Ghan, when the first northbound train pulled out of Port Augusta.

Back in Quorn, the Pichi Richi's workshop stands on the site of the century-old workshops of the South Australian and Commonwealth railways, whose disused stone-lined inspection pits remain in place. Serious enthusiasts tour the depot to admire the collection of historic locomotives, goods vans and carriages rescued from across Australia. Volunteers have restored many to working order, including NSS34, the Commonwealth Railways' deluxe Special Service Car (hired out for weddings and other functions). Other rolling stock, in varying states of repair, awaits its turn.

This morning ten historic passenger carriages, meticulously rebuilt and refurbished, are hitched up to a veteran steam locomotive, readying the Pichi Richi Explorer for the half-day excursion to Woolshed Flat, a whistle-stop halt 32km (20 miles) down the line. Philip Mellors, president of PRRPS, stands below the cab, observing a trainee who is vigorously shovelling coal. Kevin Dale will be driving W933, an ex-West Australian Government Railways W Class 4-8-2 steam locomotive built by Beyer Peacock & Co. of Manchester, around 1951.

Conductor George Wheeler, a florid-faced gentleman uniformed in black peaked cap and jacket, bellows 'Hurry up!' but there is a twinkle in his eye. We take our places in the *Lincoln* car, with its two rows of facing bench seats. Windows and shutters function perfectly, for the rolling stock has been painstakingly restored by volunteers who relish the privilege of working in the PRR workshop.

The passenger cars, some as much as a century old, are a mixed group of original South Australian Railways and Commonwealth Railways stock. The *Lincoln* is a 10.6m (35ft) 'short tom', with almost Lilliputian end canopies and steps, built for South Australia's narrow gauge railways in the early 1900s. The next car, *Wandana*, is a 15.2m (50ft) 'long tom' of similar vintage. The *Flinders*, fitted out with bedroom, toilet and glass-fronted observation area, was once a South Australian Railways commissioner's sleeping car on inspection tours.

Eighteen minutes out of Quorn, W933 summons up its reserves of steam as the train approaches the highest point of Pichi Richi Pass, at 406m (1332ft) above sea level. Deep cuttings and embankments expose the brick-red bedrock, which elsewhere peeps through a shimmering purple blush of Salvation Jane or Patterson's Curse (a tenacious weed), dotted intermittently with yellow dandelions. Spreading white trunks of River Red Gum mark the gravelly, dry creek beds. As we cross one of many bridges, Rocket the black cattle dog leaps forward, right on cue, to sprint alongside the train for the next few hundred metres.

At Woolshed Flat passengers spill out into the open beside the single building. A queue forms as the refreshment car staff dispense tea, coffee and Cornish pasties. This, the Light Car, is another former commissioner's VIP carriage once fitted with office and sleeping quarters. Meanwhile, W933 shunts around a loop to reverse the train's direction, providing a prime photo opportunity.

Two services operate full-day excursions on the full 78-km (48-mile) run between Port Augusta and Quorn. Both are steam-hauled except during the high fire-danger months of March and November. The first, originating in Port Augusta, is PRR's Afghan Express, which uses timber-bodied carriages built in the late 1920s for the old narrow gauge Ghan service. The original Afghan Express ran from Terowie northbound through Quorn in 1923. The train acquired its unusual moniker from an Afghan camel driver who alighted at Quorn to recite his evening prayers. Local wits dubbed the train the Afghan Express, and, over time, this became enshrined as The Ghan. The second full-day service, which runs southward from Quorn, is PRR's Transcontinental, which takes its name from the trans-Australian service operated on the standard gauge line from Port Augusta westwards from 1917 onward.

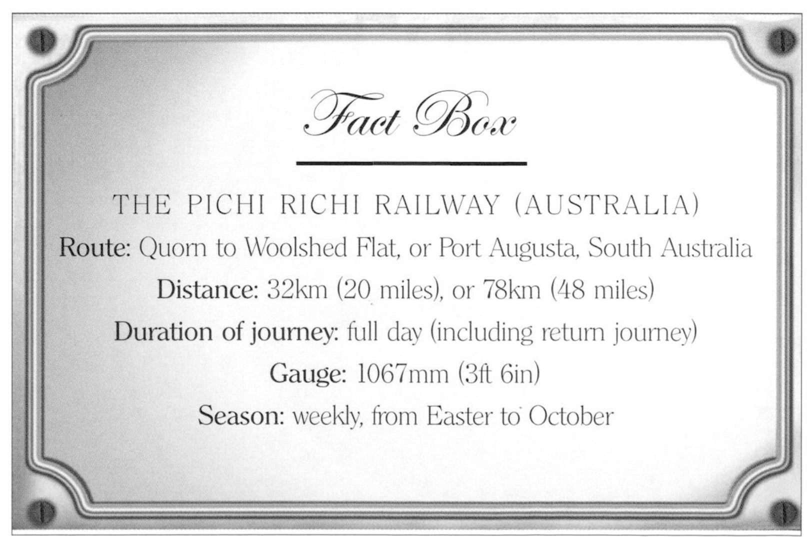

Fact Box

THE PICHI RICHI RAILWAY (AUSTRALIA)

Route: Quorn to Woolshed Flat, or Port Augusta, South Australia

Distance: 32km (20 miles), or 78km (48 miles)

Duration of journey: full day (including return journey)

Gauge: 1067mm (3ft 6in)

Season: weekly, from Easter to October

Contact and booking information

ALBERTA PRAIRIE STEAM TOURS (CANADA)
Alberta Prairie Railway Excursions, PO Box 1600, Stettler, AL T0C 2L0, Canada
Tel: +1 (403) 742-2811 (outside Alberta) or 1-800-282-3994 (in Alberta)
Fax: +1 (403) 742-2844
Email: info@absteamtrain.com
Website: www.absteamtrain.com/

HULL–CHELSEA–WAKEFIELD STEAM TRAIN (CANADA)
Hull–Chelsea–Wakefield Steam Train, 165 Deveault Street, Gatineau, QC J8Z 1S7, Canada
Tel: +1 (819) 778-7246
Fax: +1 (819) 778-5007
Email: info@steamtrain.ca
Website: www.steamtrain.ca

CASS SCENIC RAILROAD (UNITED STATES)
Cass Scenic Railroad State Park, PO Box 107, Cass, WV 24927, USA
Tel: +1 (304) 456-4300 or 1-800-CALL WVA (within USA)
Fax: +1 (304) 456-4641
Email: cassrr@sunlitsurf.com
Website: www.cassrailroad.com

GRAND CANYON RAILWAY (UNITED STATES)
Grand Canyon Railway, 233 N. Grand Canyon Blvd. Williams, AZ 86046, USA
Tel: +1-800-843-8724
Fax: +1 (928) 773-1610
Email: info@thetrain.com
Website: www.thetrain.com

STEAMTOWN NATIONAL HISTORIC SITE (UNITED STATES)
Steamtown National Historic Site, 150 South Washington Avenue, Scranton, PA 18503-2018, USA
Tel: +1 (570) 340-5204 (reservations); +1 (570) 340-5206 (visitor information)
Fax: +1 (570) 340-5235
Email: STEA_Interpretation@nps.gov
Website: www.nps.gov/stea/

MOUNT WASHINGTON COG RAILWAY (UNITED STATES)
Mount Washington Cog Railway, Route 302, Bretton Woods, Mount Washington, NH 03589, USA
Tel: +1 (800) 922-8825; or +1 (603) 278-5404 in New Hampshire
Fax: +1 (603) 278-5830
Email: via website interface
Website: www.thecog.com

GUAYAQUIL & QUITO RAILROAD (ECUADOR)
At time of writing, there are no regularly scheduled steam tours over the Devil's Nose. Tours are run on an irregular basis, depending on the condition of the line. Readers are advised to contact one of the specialist rail tour companies for further details.

THE OLD PATAGONIA EXPRESS (ARGENTINA)
Oficina Central del Viejo Expreso Patagónico-La Trochita, Estación El Maitén (9210)
El Maitén – Provincia del Chubut, Argentina
Tel: +54 (02945) 495190
Email: turismai@epuyen.net.ar
Website: latrochita.org.ar

FFESTINIOG RAILWAY (UNITED KINGDOM)
Ffestiniog Railway, Harbour Station, Porthmadog, Gwynedd, LL49 9NF, United Kingdom
Tel: +44 (0)1766 516024
Fax: +44 (0)1766 516006
Email: info@festrail.co.uk
Website: www.ffestiniograilway.org.uk

NORTH YORKSHIRE MOORS RAILWAY (UNITED KINGDOM)
North Yorkshire Moors Railway, Pickering Station, Pickering, North Yorkshire YO18 7AJ, United Kingdom
Tel: +44 (0)1751 472508; +44 (0)1751 473535 (automated timetable)
Fax: +44 (0)1751 476970
Email: admin@nymrpickering.fsnet.co.uk
Website: www.nymr.demon.co.uk

ROMNEY, HYTHE & DYMCHURCH RAILWAY (UNITED KINGDOM)
Romney, Hythe & Dymchurch Railway, New Romney Station, New Romney, Kent TN28 8P, United Kingdom
Tel: +44 (0)1797 362353
Fax: +44 (0)1797 363591
Email: bookings@rhdr.org.uk
Website: www.rhdr.org.uk

CHEMIN DE FER DE LA BAIE DE SOMME (FRANCE)
Chemin de Fer de la Baie de Somme, BP 31, St. Valery-s/Somme 80230, France
Tel: +33 03 22 26 96 96
Fax: +33 03 22 26 95 66
Email: CFBS@neuronnexion.fr
Website: www.chemin-fer-baie-somme.asso.fr

LE TRAIN DES PIGNES (FRANCE)
Chemins de Fer de Provence, 4 bis rue Alfred Binet, 06000 Nice, France
Tel: +33 04 97 03 80 80
Fax: +33 04 97 03 80 81
Email: gecp@libertysurf.fr
Website: www.chez.com/gecp/tv/tvhoraires.html

DAMPFBAHN FURKA-BERGSTRECKE (SWITZERLAND)
Dampfbahn Furka-Bergstrecke AG, Postfach 35, CH-3999 Oberwald, Switzerland
Tel: +41 848 000 144
Fax: +41 55 615 3093
Email: reisedienst@fu-be.ch
Website: www.furka-bergstrecke.ch

BAD DOBERAN–KÜHLUNGSBORN WEST (GERMANY)
Mecklenburgischen Bäderbahn Molli Gmbh. & Co. KG Erstellt., Am Bahnhof, D-18209 Bad Doberan, Germany
Tel: +49 038203/415-0
Fax: +49 038203/415-12
Email: molli-bahn@t-online.de
Website: www.molli-bahn.de

RÜGENSCHE KLEINBAHN (GERMANY)
Rügensche Kleinbahn GmbH. & Co., Binzer Straße 12, D-18581 Putbus, Germany
Tel: +49 038301/801-12
Fax: +49 038301/801-15
Email: info@rasender-roland.de
Website: www.rasender-roland.de

WOLSZTYN TO POZNAN (POLAND)
The Wolsztyn Experience, 20 Whitepit Lane, Flackwell Heath, High Wycombe, Buckinghamshire HP10 9HS, United Kingdom;
or UL Gajewskich 4A, 64-200 Wolsztyn, Poland
Tel/Fax: +44 (0)1628 524876
Website: www.bucksrailcentre.org.uk/poland.htm

OSTRA SODERMANLANDS JARNVAG (SWEDEN)
Östra Södermanlands Järnväg, Box 53, SE-647 22 Mariefred, Sweden
Tel: +46 0159-21000
Fax: +46 0159-21115
Email: oslj@telia.com
Website: www.oslj.nu/indexgb.html

THE SETESDALSBANEN (NORWAY)
Stiftelsen Setesdalsbanen, Grovane, N-4700 Venessla, Norway
Tel: +47 3815 6482
Fax: +47 3815 6721
Email: post@setesdalsbanen.no
Website: www.setesdalsbanen.no/index_en.html

RAILWAY REVIVAL IN THE HORN OF AFRICA (ERITREA)
Railway Touring Company, 14 Tuesday Market Place, PO Box 1012, Kings Lynn, Norfolk PE30 3YN, United Kingdom
Tel: +44 (0)1553 661500
Fax: +44 (0)1553 661800
Email: n.dobbing@btconnect.com
Website: www.railwaytouring.co.uk
Enthusiast Holidays, 146 Forest Hill Rd., London SE23 3QR, United Kingdom
Tel: +44 (0)20 8699 3654 (or +44 (0)1354 660222/660555)
Fax: +44 (0)20 8291 6496
Email: info@enthusiasthols.com
Website: www.enthusiasthols.com
Gunter Oczko Dampfsafaris, Am Sudhang 2, D-53809, Ruppichteroth, Germany
Email: Oczko.winterscheid@t-online.de

BANANA EXPRESS (SOUTH AFRICA)
Port Shepstone & Alfred County Railway Co. Ltd., PO Box 852, Port Shepstone 4240, South Africa
Tel: +27 (0) 39 682 4821 (office hours), or (0) 39 695 0520 (all hours and faxes)
+27 (0) 72 112 1136 (mobile)
Email: acrailmc@venturenet.co.za
Website: www.bananaexpress.co.za

OUTENIQUA CHOO-TJOE (SOUTH AFRICA)
Outeniqua Transport Museum, 2 Mission Street, George 6529, South Africa
Tel: +27 (0) 44 801-8288; +27 (0) 44 801-8289
Fax: +27 (0) 44 801-8286
Email: info@onlinesources.co.za
Website: www.onlinesources.co.za/chootjoe/index.html

HEDJAZ RAILWAY (SYRIA/JORDAN)
The Railway Touring Company, 14 Tuesday Market Place, PO Box 1012, King's Lynn, Norfolk PE30 3YN, United Kingdom
Tel: +44 (0)1553 661500
Fax: 01553 661800
Email: enquiries@railwaytouring.co.uk
Website: www.railwaytouring.co.uk

CHANGA MANGA FOREST RAILWAY (PAKISTAN)
Divisional Forest Manager, Changa Manga Forest, Changa Manga, Punjab, Pakistan
Tel: +92 04951 381023/381417

ZIG ZAG RAILWAY (AUSTRALIA)
Zig Zag Railway Co-op. Ltd., PO Box 1, Lithgow, NSW 2790, Australia
Tel: +61 (0)2 6353 1795 (business hours, weekdays); +61 (0)2 6351 4826 (recorded timetable)
Fax: +61 (0)2 6353 1801
Email: zigzag@pnc.com.au
Website: www.zigzagrailway.com.au

PICHI RICHI RAILWAY (AUSTRALIA)
Pichi Richi Railway, PO Box 111, Quorn SA 5433, Australia
Tel: +61 (0)8 8648 6598; +61 0(8) 8395 2566 (recorded timetable)
Fax: +61 (0)8 8648 6181
Email: info@prr.org.au; bookings@prr.org.au
Website: www.prr.org.au/timetable.php

DISCLAIMER
The information presented here is based on suggestions of the authors and on research done by the Publisher, and was correct at date of publication. The information provided is in no way an endorsement of any of the listed parties. Details such as telephone and fax numbers, email addresses and URLs are subject to change. The Publisher can accept no liability arising from the use of information presented here.

LEFT *A freight train pulls out of Wolsztyn junction. Thanks to the unique Wolsztyn Experience (see details above), steam enthusiasts can travel to Poland to get hands-on driving experience.*

About the authors

ANTHONY LAMBERT

ANTHONY LAMBERT, consultant editor and author, has written 15 books on railways and travel, including *Explore Britain's Steam Railways* and *Switzerland by Rail.* He contributed to the AA's *Train Journeys of the World, Insight Guide to Great Railway Journeys of Europe* and *Insight Guide to Pakistan.* He has also written for the *New York Times, Daily Telegraph, Sunday Times, Wanderlust* and the *Orient-Express Magazine*, was consultant editor to the nine-volume partwork *The World of Trains*, and a contributing author to *The World's Great Railway Journeys* (New Holland, 2001) and *Extraordinary Railway Journeys* (New Holland, 2004). He is a trustee of the Birmingham Railway Museum and the Kidderminster Railway Museum.

PAUL ASH

PAUL ASH saw his first steam locomotive when he was three years old – a squat shunting engine in a lakeside yard south of Johannesburg. Too young to go sailing with the rest of the family, his weekends thereafter were spent staring through the fence at steam engines on the shunt. It probably helped that his father and grandfather were for half a century the South African agents for Henschel, Germany's greatest steam locomotive builders. The house was always full of railway books, engineering drawings and photographs of Henschel locomotives belting across the Karoo desert with heavy freights and crack passenger trains. But although the love of steam was handed down over the generations, an affinity for mathematics was not, ruling out a career in engineering. Fortunately, journalism has provided an outlet, allowing him to travel the world looking for lost steam locomotives and backwoods train journeys, on one of which he met his wife. He has authored two travel guides, one on rail travel in Africa, and remains open to any suggestion of running for the next train and riding it to the end of the line.

STEVE BARRY

STEVE BARRY's interest in trains started when he was growing up in southern New Jersey. Summer evenings were spent with his father watching commuter trains coming into his hometown, Millville, from the Philadelphia suburb of Camden. Weekends were spent on day trips to the Strasburg Rail Road or on the Reading's legendary Iron Horse Rambles. After graduating from Rutgers University in 1979, Steve started his full-time railfanning (at least on weekends) by attending that year's National Railway Historical Society (NRHS) Convention in Washington, DC. Since then he has attended every NRHS gathering, and he later became the National Director for the NRHS Wilmington, Delaware, Chapter, and NRHS Eastern Region Vice President. Steve's contributions to the rail hobby press started with an article in *Rail Classics* in 1983. In 1986 he submitted his first article to *Railpace Newsmagazine*. In 1996 he joined *Railfan & Railroad* as associate editor and was made managing editor a year later. Steve was also a contributing author to New Holland's *The World's Great Railway Journeys* (2001) and *Extraordinary Railway Journeys* (2004).

Steve will shoot anything on rails, from CSX's latest power to streetcars and tourist steam, and estimates that he has taken about 100,000 slides in 12 years of photography.

COLIN BOOCOCK

COLIN BOOCOCK has nearly 50 years' experience in traction and rolling stock engineering as a career railwayman, and has been a railway enthusiast and traveller all of his life. He has developed a keen interest in all types of railways in as many countries as he can spare the time (and cash) to visit. Not content to build up a collection of photographs for his own interest, Colin likes to share these with a wider audience. He is also a prolific writer of illustrated articles and has written 15 railway books to date. He was also a contributing author to *The World's Great Railway Journeys* (New Holland, 2001) and *Extraordinary Railway Journeys* (New Holland, 2004).

His photographs cover more than 55 years of railways and travel. He still visits new countries and distant places, choosing train travel whenever possible. 'I am in my natural and most relaxed environment in a train!'

AILSA CAMM

AILSA CAMM was born in the Netherlands to British parents; her experience of rail travel began with the journey to school, on Holland's first electrified railway line and along the route of the fabled Blue Tram to The Hague. She has contributed articles to newspapers, magazines and travel guides in the UK and abroad.

However, much as she enjoys being a passenger, she firmly believes that the best place to travel – at least on a steam train – is in the cab. In pursuit of that goal, she has attended a driver's and fireman's course and recently drove one of the last surviving steam-hauled passenger services at Wolsztyn in Poland. She lives and works in Surrey.

PHILIP GAME

PHILIP GAME has been a keen traveller since student days in the early 1970s. He has distant memories of a seventh-birthday excursion aboard the long-defunct Tasmanian Railways in 1959.

As Australian vice-consul in the United Arab Emirates, Philip had the opportunity to explore remote regions of eastern Arabia (where there are, unfortunately, no railways). He has also worked as a guide in Malaysia and Thailand, leading small groups touring by bus, communal taxi, longboat, elephant and of course, train. In 1995 the Games travelled widely in the USA, living and working in Pennsylvania. More recently, living near London, they experienced at first hand the plight of Britain's privatized railways.

Philip Game's travel writing career was launched with the story of his experiences riding the now-defunct

Forsayth Mixed Goods 7A90 through the Queensland Outback in 1992. His articles have since been published in 30 countries. He was a contributing author to *The World's Great Railway Journeys* (New Holland, 2001) and *Extraordinary Railway Journeys* (New Holland, 2004).

PIERRE HOME-DOUGLAS

PIERRE HOME-DOUGLAS worked for 13 years as a book editor in Montreal, where he lives with his wife and two daughters. He has written chapters for a half dozen travel books, as well as articles for numerous Canadian and American magazines and newspapers on subjects including gliding, bicycling through Vermont, sailing up the Nile, and canoeing in the northern woods of Canada. His chapter on the trans-continental Canadian train appeared in *The World's Great Railway Journeys* (New Holland, 2001).

PETER LEMMEY

PETER LEMMEY developed a taste for rail travel early in life on the Atlantic Coast Express. Family holidays in Europe in the 1960s opened up the interesting possibility of thorough exploration 'off the beaten track' by train, spurred on by writers such as Bryan Morgan and PB Whitehouse, who tempted many an intrepid traveller to cross the Channel to see for himself.

In 1980 he made the first of many visits to the Indian subcontinent, where he explored by train some of the more remote and less-visited parts of India and Pakistan. In both countries, his journeys were made more enjoyable and rewarding through the hospitality of local railwaymen and by the cooperation of railway administrators in furnishing him with permission for rides on the engines themselves, as well as finding railway accommodation in out-of-the-way spots and, on one or two occasions, even special trains.

Peter has contributed a number of articles about exotic train journeys to the travel press, and was a contributing author to New Holland's *The World's Great Railway Journeys* (2001) and *Extraordinary Railway Journeys* (2004).

NICK LERA

NICK LERA is a TV documentary producer specializing in overseas railways. His subjects have included the Khyber Pass, the South American Andes and the Hedjaz Railway. An ex-BBC cameraman, he has filmed in many war zones, including Vietnam, and twice received the coveted News Cameraman Of The Year Award, in 1969 and 1970. In 1980 he worked as director/cameraman on BBC-TV's original *Great Railway Journeys of the World* series.

JOHN PARKER

JOHN PARKER is a retired company chairman whose lifelong love of steam locomotives has taken him all over the world. He is particularly fascinated by the ways railways integrate into society and their effect on the day-to-day lives

of railwaymen A keen photographer, he has used formats from 35mm to 6x7. He now uses DV.CAM as his preferred medium for capturing the sights and sounds of locomotives hard at work.

CARL G. PERELMAN

CARL G. PERELMAN is the news editor of *Railpace Newsmagazine*, which covers the Northeast US and Eastern Canada. He was born in Newark, NJ, and grew up in nearby Union, NJ. His railroad photography began in 1974, with visits to nearby railroad yards and depots. His first photo was published on the cover of *Trains Magazine* when he was 16 years old. In 1982 he graduated from the American University in Washington, DC, and subsequently completed graduate work at New York University. He and his family live in suburban New Jersey.

SUSAN STORM

SUSAN STORM is a travel writer and photographer, finding the beautiful, the unusual and the confronting from Amorgos to Zanzibar. She has ridden iconic trains in South America, India, Australia, Thailand, New Zealand and Europe and lived to tell their tales, but was astonished to discover the Zig Zag Railway, with its important history,

almost in her Sydney back yard. She so enjoyed the short but exhilarating experience that she went back again the following weekend, wondering if there was an opening for a volunteer weekend female coal shoveller. Fortunately, there wasn't, so she's staying with writing.

MICHAEL WHITEHOUSE

MICHAEL WHITEHOUSE has travelled the world in search of steam trains in interesting and obscure places and has a large collection of historic and modern railway photographs. He is chairman of Millbrook House Limited, which operates a railway picture library with access to the well known Railway Roundabout collection. He participates actively in the railway preservation movement in the UK, being Chairman of the Ffestiniog and Welsh Highland Railway Companies and its associated travel company, Ffestiniog Travel.
He is also Chairman of the Birmingham Railway Museum Trust. This fits well with his career as a rail project lawyer and partner in the law firm Wragge & Co, where he has advised clients on a wide range of railway projects ranging from the Virgin Cross Country tilting trains, the London Underground PPP, the privatization of Zambia and Kenya Railways and UK passenger franchising.

Index

Photographic credits

Copyright rests with the following photographers and/or their agents.

Key to abbreviations:
Paul Ash = PA
Bob Avery = BA
Steve Barry = SB
Jürgen Bogelspacher = JB
Colin Boocock = CB
Philip Game = PG
Peter Groom = PGR
Chris Hinton = CH
Pierre Home-Douglas = PHD
David Idle = DI
Anthony J. Lambert = AL
Peter Lemmey = PL
Nick Lera = NL
Frank Neubauer = FN
Bernd Seiler = BS
Steamtown National Historic Site = SNHS
Susan Storm = SS
John Tickner = JT
Michael Whitehouse = MW

Key to locations: top = t; bottom = b; left = l; right = r

Page	Location	Credit
front cover		JT
back cover		BS
back flap		RR Bridgewater
endpapers		BS
p1		JT
pp2–3		MW
pp4–5		SS
pp6–7		SB
pp8–9		Milepost 92½
pp10–11		SB
pp12–13		BS
pp14–15		Donald Wilson
pp16–17		SB
p18		AL
pp18–19		Bob Willis
pp20–1		AL
p22		PHD
pp22–3		PHD
pp24	bl	PHD
pp24	br	PHD
p25	bl	PHD
p26		NL
pp26–7		NL
pp28–9		SB
p30		JB
pp30–1		SB
p32		SB
p34		SNHS
pp34–5		SB
pp36–7		SB
pp38–9		SNHS
p40		SB
pp40–1		SB
p42		SB
p44		MW
pp44–5		MW
p46		JB
p47		MW
p48		John E. Parker
p49		JB
p50		JB
pp50–1		Carl G. Perelman
p52		MW
p53		MW
pp54–5		BS
p56		MW
pp56–7		BA
p58		MW
p60		AL
pp60–1		BA
pp62–3		DI
p64		DI
p65		DI
pp66–7		BA
p68		PGR
pp68–9		PGR
p71		PGR
p72		MW
pp72–3		PL
p74		PL
p75		MW
p76		MW
pp76–7		PL
p79		Jean-Daniel Paré
p80		JB
pp80–1		JB
p82		Beat Moser
p83		JB
p84		JB
pp84–5		CB
pp86–7		CB
p88		FN
pp88–9		AL
p90		AL
p91		FN
p92		BS
pp92–3		BS
pp94–5		BS
pp96–7		BS
p98		BS
p99		BS
p100		MW
pp100–1		MW
p102	bl	MW
p102	br	MW
p103	bl	MW
p103	br	MW
p104		CH
pp104–5		CH
pp106–7		CH
pp108–9		PL
p110		NL
pp110–11		NL
pp112–13		NL
p113		NL
p114		NL
pp114–15		NL
p115		NL
p116		NL
p117		NL
p118		NL
p119		NL
p120		PA
pp120–1		PA
p122		MW
p124		MW
pp124–5		JT
p126		CB
p127		CB
pp128–9		AL
p130		MW
pp130–1		MW
p132		AL
p133		AL
pp134–5		AL
pp136–7		AL
p138		AL
pp138–9		PL
pp140–1		PL
p142		AL
p143		AL
pp144–5		SS
pp146		SS
pp146–7		SS
p148		SS
p150		PG
pp150–1		PG
p152		PG
p153		PG
pp154–5		BS

Acknowledgements

The Publisher would like to thank the following people for their assistance in producing this book: Vic Allen, Enthusiast Holidays; Gus Annas; Melodie Averna, Hull–Chelsea–Wakefield Steam Train; Mandi Butterly; Bill Clark, Steamtown National Historic Site; Kathryn Dingle, Michael Helmerich; Louise Hounsell; Roland Minder; Beatrice Schwarz; Mel Traest; Oliver Ueck; Bob Willis, Alberta Prairie Railway Excursions.